FRANCIS & EDITH SCHAEFFER

EVANGELICAL WARRIORS

by

SAM WELLMAN

PILLARS OF THE FAITH SERIES

from

WILD CENTURIES PRESS

WILD CENTURIES PRESS
www.wildcenturies.com

Copyright © 2000 Sam Wellman
Copyright © 2013 Sam Wellman

ISBN-13: 978-0-9897905-2-9

Typefaces: Book Antiqua, Gill Sans MT

Chapter I

Bessie Schaeffer woke up with a start.

"Go get the doctor!" she yelled to her slumbering husband Frank.

Frank rushed out in the middle of night into the chill winter air. Bessie tried to calm herself, although each contraction startled her. This was her first child. Soon the doctor arrived, bleary-eyed and wobbly. 'Is he drunk?' worried Bessie. Drunk or not, the doctor tied one end of a sheet to the footboard of the bed and commanded Bessie to pull on the other end of the sheet with her arms while she contracted her stomach muscles.

Later she gushed, "It was easy. I just pulled on the sheet and pushed, and the baby was there on the bed!"[1]

Thus, baby Francis August Schaeffer - eager, it seemed - was born January 30, 1912, in his parents' home. Toddler 'Fran' learned soon enough he lived in a suburb of Philadelphia called 'Germantown'. His father Frank was American-born but indeed of German descent. It had been Fran's grandfather Franz Schaeffer, long dead, and his wife Carolina, still alive in 1912, who came to America from Germany. On the other side, Fran's mother was of British descent but born Bessie Williamson in America. Grandfather Williamson was dead, but grandmother Mary Williamson was still very much alive. In fact, Mary's father William Joyce, an immigrant from England, was also still alive - at 96.

"Your great grandfather died not long after you were born," explained Fran's mother later. "He was a mailman. Everyone called him 'Uncle Billy'."

The Frank Schaeffers lived on Pastorius Street, not far off Germantown Avenue, the town's main street. Little 'Fran' soon romped around a tiny front lawn, enclosed within a wrought-iron fence. In a grass-starved area under a lilac bush Fran energetically scooped dirt into his tiny bucket, then dumped it. All day long the street reverberated with horse-drawn carts. One moment would bring a scissors grinder, another a fishmonger and another a vegetable cart. Fran soon learned to anxiously await the 'waffle man' with his

---

[1] Edith Schaeffer, *The Tapestry: The Life and Times of of Francis and Edith Schaeffer*. (Waco, Texas: Word Books, 1981), 37.

1

buttery, sugary delights. At dusk Fran was inside the house at the front window, watching the lamplighter ascend his step ladder to light the gas street lights.

Mother Bessie often said emphatically, "I'm not going to be a slave to children."[1]

Fran only understood the consequences of that attitude later. He never had a brother or a sister. Perhaps he was lucky to have been born at all. Grandfather Williamson had died when Bessie was only eight. Bessie became the 'little mother' of the other three children - washing, ironing and cooking for many years. Bessie's attitude was only reinforced by Fran's father Frank. He too had taken on adult responsibilities as a child because his father died when he was only three.

"By the age of ten I had a steady job at the local coal mine," Frank reminded Fran, "where I straddled a conveyer belt all day long - culling rocks from the coal!"

In any event it seemed to Fran that his parents could not have worked any harder than they did. Mother had a work routine in the house rarely ever interrupted by leisure. Monday was 'wash day'. Frank began the day by filling the wash tubs with hot water before leaving for work. Because of the lean days of her own childhood Bessie was used to making soap from scraps of animal fat and drippings. She boiled the fat with lye until white soap miraculously accumulated on top. For laundering she shaved slivers off her bars of soap and stirred them into the hot water. After kneading the dirty clothes in the hot, soapy water, perhaps after rubbing the bar of soap over stubborn stains, she worked the clothes over her corrugated washboard. Of course all the laundry then had to be rinsed and hung on lines to dry. Certain items were dipped into a starch mixture before drying. Meticulous Bessie mixed two strengths of starch.

"Table clothes, napkins and my aprons get a light mixture," she told a barely comprehending Fran, "But the collars and cuffs of your father's shirts get a thicker mixture."

After all the items were dry, Bessie sprinkled them with water and rolled them. On Tuesday Bessie spread a padded blanket over the large oak dining table, then spread a sheet over that. This was her 'ironing board'. Several heavy flatirons were kept hot on the stovetop. Bessie would insert her wooden handle in one, then

---

[1] Schaeffer, *Tapestry*, 37.

tirelessly run the iron over item after item of clothing until the iron was too cool. Then a fresh flatiron replaced it. All day Bessie did this until the ironing was done. Wednesday was for mending and sewing. Buttons were sewn back on, hems repaired and holes mended. Sewing was tedious but not exhausting. Bessie sat in her rocking chair. After mending she preceded on her never-ending sewing projects of new clothing. On Thursday Bessie trudged to the markets on Germantown Avenue, buying groceries that were not offered by the street vendors. When Fran was little more than a toddler he pulled his first large wagon to the markets. On the way home his wagon was much harder to pull.

"Don't spill any groceries," warned his stern mother.

Friday was a hard day. Bessie covered her hair with a scarf and cleaned. It seemed she dusted every surface in the house. She polished the furniture and swept the rugs. Once a week she went to her mother's house to help clean her house. Of course Bessie did spring and fall housecleaning too. At these times the Schaeffers carried outside all the mattresses to be aired and all the carpets to be beaten. When Fran's father was home he was as busy as Bessie. If Bessie had discovered a problem with the plumbing or gas lighting or a jammed window Frank would fix it. He was as handy in the house as he was on his paying jobs, for he was a 'handyman' with a reputation as a no-nonsense worker who could troubleshoot a balky elevator or a steam engine. Frank was a naval veteran, even serving on a warship called a 'monitor' during the Spanish-American War. No mechanical problem intimidated him. Gas lighting was pleasant, yet Frank was one of the first in Germantown to wire his house for electricity. And it seemed no time at all before little Fran was helping 'Pop' and learning how to use all his tools, even the saw.

"Now, don't get your clothes dirty," Bessie would say.

'No-nonsense' would describe Bessie very well. In fact, without other children Fran grew up in very sober, very hardworking, very quiet house. They attended an evangelical church. Bessie belonged to their ladies' society, often rolling and folding bandages or sewing clothing to send abroad through a missionary society. Frank found little peace in church. He had bitter memories of another church he attended as a child. He had been treated like one of the 'poor kids'. As a mine-worker at 10 Frank considered the soft-handed pastor - not himself - a ward of society.

"The pastor didn't know what work was; he just stood up there and talked," grumbled Frank.[1]

The hardworking Schaeffers had moments of relaxation too. Milder events were making ice cream or icing down a fat watermelon on a hot summer day. More exciting were shooting off fireworks or hiking through nearby Fairmont Park or something really momentous like going all the way to Atlantic City. The family rode an early morning trolley east to the Delaware River, crossed the river on a ferry, then rode a train all the way across New Jersey to Atlantic City. In the evening they returned to Germantown.

'But not before we strolled the boardwalk and the beach,' reflected Fran, remembering the Atlantic Ocean, 'in our heavy woolen swimsuits!'

Fran did not feel deprived in such a household. He was rather proud of his parents. Mother was tall and sturdy, very nice looking in her rolled-back hair. Father was good-looking too, clean shaven with short cropped hair. He was broad-shouldered, with rolled up sleeves exposing work-hardened arms. And although Fran's parents had both worked very hard in their childhood they gave Fran only chores to do when he was not in school. His most difficult chore was taking his wagon once a week to the icehouse one mile away. Then he lugged home a huge block of ice for the icebox. But he loved the freedom of the outing. And he had two grandmothers in the neighborhood who spoiled him. His grade school was a mile away from home. Because one of the grandmothers lived only half a block from the grade school Fran ate lunch there every day.

It was this grandmother's never-failing, light-hearted generosity that first made Fran realize his mother Bessie had a hard edge to her. Occasionally Bessie was cruel. Once when she was taking a very excited Fran to church to recite a poem in a Christmas program he fell and tore a hole in his stocking. His outing turned into a nightmare. Mother hustled him back home to a good spanking - she used a leather strap Fran's father had to sharpen his straight razor - and a change of stockings. Then Fran was hustled to church to recite his poem. He performed well but it was not a memory he cherished. Ironically his father never used the leather strap to punish Fran. All his father had to do was show his disappointment in Fran.

"Francis...," his father would say through tight lips.

And Fran was crestfallen.

---

[1] Schaeffer, *Tapestry*, 26.

School was rough, inside and outside. Teachers did not hesitate to strike unruly children. Fran was struck often. Often on impulse Fran was wild. Rolling apples up the aisles to the teacher's desk was a custom. One day amid sounds of apples thumping up the wooden floors was a resounding whack. Fran's apple had careened off the chalkboard behind the teacher's head! Fortunately for Fran the teacher did not know the source of the missile. Another of his small rebellions was when he ducked the teacher's fist and she struck a bench behind him. Her yowl of pain more than compensated for the whipping he got. The playground was a series of wars too. Although small for his age Fran was not picked on often. He never avoided a scrap. And he was ferocious. His most lasting wound was from a peashooter. The pea struck him so hard in the cheek it embedded itself. It left a tiny scar. Schoolwork was very easy for Fran but he saw little use for it. As far as he was concerned they didn't teach him anything practical like wiring a house for electricity or making one of the new-fangled radios. His 'undereducated' father could do those marvelous things. Wondrous things were happening in the world - automobiles, airplanes, even world war - but they seemed unrelated to school. Still, the teachers seemed particularly interested in his future education. He had taken some tests at school. What had they revealed? His parents would not tell him.

"Yet my parents talked for a while about sending me to Germantown Academy," he remembered later.

By the end of grade school Fran was a normal 'rough and ready' boy. He careened down hills in his wagon. In the winter he flopped onto his Flexible Flyer sled and slalomed headfirst down snowy hillsides. Once he bottomed out onto a frozen pond, slithering wildly. He broke through the ice! But this was not the tragedy it might have been. The water was only knee deep. Still, it was a bone-chilling walk home. His most serious childhood illness was scarlet fever. In those days a serious contagious disease caused a house to be 'quarantined'. A man from the health board appeared and hammered a white cardboard placard on the front door. 'SCARLET FEVER,' screamed the placard! Only a health officer could remove the placard. For several days Fran's fever triggered hallucinations of monsters. Occasionally he was coherent enough to recognize his mother making him drink a glass of water. Oh, how wonderful water tasted! He remembered a face peering anxiously in his bedroom window.

5

"Hi, Pop," yelled Fran in a moment of recognition.

At eleven Fran entered Roosevelt Junior High School. Mrs. Lidie C. Bell, who was also his 'home room' teacher, impressed him with her classes in art appreciation and drawing. It seemed his first experience with fine art. About this same time Fran joined the Boy Scouts. He had just the right aggression for pursuing merit badges. He also represented his troop in a speech contest and won. The cup was engraved "Pyramid Club Cup Four Minute Speech Contest Won by Francis A. Schaeffer, Troop 38, 1923".[1] His scout troop met at the First Presbyterian Church of Germantown. Soon Fran and his parents were attending this church. Fran's parents were stern but they indulged him. They bought him a membership in the YMCA where he learned to swim and perform basic gymnastics. They started him in piano lessons too. In frustration he quit the lessons. He was even dismissed from the scout band where he had nothing more difficult to do than clang the cymbals. He had no aptitude whatever for music.

'Perhaps,' he thought, 'I have no aptitude for the finer things in life.'

The summer of 1925 brought America the 'Monkey Trial'. A high school biology teacher in Tennessee was being prosecuting for teaching evolution. It ballooned into a great national event because the prosecution enlisted Williams Jennings Bryan, a politician noted for his oratory. The defense enlisted Clarence Darrow, a famous defense attorney. Besides being in very bad health Bryan was ineffective in the format of a jury trial. Darrow was not only in his element but an atheist. He ridiculed the Bible with relish and although he lost the case the liberal newspapers covering the trial glorified him. Fran heard murmurs in his church that the trial was a great loss for religious fundamentalism.

"Whatever 'fundamentalism' is," he shrugged.

In school Fran steered away from college preparation courses. He focussed on vocational shop courses. Surely mechanical drawing, woodworking, electrical studies and forging metal would prepare him for the real world - the world his father excelled in. Fran seemed destined to follow his father's path. He had wiggled through the attic laying electric wires for his father. With his father he had put in wooden floors. He had painted inside and out, built a garage, layed brick, mended gutters on the roof, built a coal bin in

---

[1] Schaeffer, *Tapestry*, 46.

the cellar, plumbed, poured concrete and done a dozen other skillful things. By the time Fran started Germantown High School the Schaeffers had moved to a much larger house on Ross Street. It too was a 'fixer upper'.

"What are we going to fix first, Pop?" asked Fran, assuming he would help his father on that house too.

Yet Fran was very active outside the home too. As well as scout activity he belonged to the Rifle Club, played basketball once a week at the church, roller skated at the local rinks and tackled tougher and tougher shop projects. He also joined a fraternity. He was taken with all the other pledges to a vacant lot, where amid hoots and howls the members covered them with molasses and bird seed. Suddenly the police arrived. The members scattered, leaving the confused pledges to fend for themselves. The police were not amused and hauled the pledges to the police station in a paddy wagon. There it was Fran who made an impassioned appeal for mercy to the desk sergeant.

The sergeant waved them out. "Don't do that again!"

Fran was now of an age to take Saturday jobs. First he worked with a street fishmonger, who had Fran screaming 'Fish! Fresh Fish!' at the top of his lungs. Then Fran helped the fishmonger fill the baskets of women when they came to the fish cart from their houses. But his employer was so cruel to his horse Fran could not bear it very long. He quit. His next Saturday job was at a meat market at Reading Terminal, an hour's trolley ride from home. For 12 grueling hours Fran unpacked meat in the ice room or helped deliver it to smaller markets. He took another job where he had to enter steam boilers to chip away scale with hammer and chisel. In yet another job he worked at the icehouse loading 200-pound blocks of ice into wagons. In a far less strenuous venture, at home he made beaded flowers that women wore as pins. For a while he sold these to department stores.

'And all around me the world is just bristling with excitement,' marveled Fran.

Charles Lindbergh's feat of flying across the Atlantic Ocean alone was all the news the summer of 1927 when Fran was 15. The next year brought demonstrations of not only colored motion pictures but also television! But the summers of 1929, 1930 and 1931 were fabled for Philadelphia. Their baseball team, the Philadelphia Athletics - led by the batting of Jimmy Foxx and Al Simmons and the pitching of Lefty Grove and George Earnshaw - wrenched the pennant from the Yankees, supposedly invincible with Babe Ruth and Lou Gehrig. Not only did the A's conquer the Yankees but they went on to win the World Series two of those summers! The great red-brick, multi-tiered rectangle, Shibe Park, was an easy trolley ride from Germantown.

Oh, it was a great time to live in the sweep of Philadelphia!

By the time Fran was 17 and a junior in high school he attended church and Sunday School, but he doubted the truth of everything he heard. One day however his Sunday School teacher asked Fran to help a Russian immigrant learn English. Fran was so inexperienced at that kind of thing he came home from Philadelphia's famous bookstore Leary's not with a Russian-English book but a book on Greek philosophy! Grumbling at his wasted journey he began to read the book anyway. The ideas exploded in his head! Here were people actually trying to unravel the essence of life. Fran couldn't put the book down. But try as he might he found no satisfaction in the answers philosophers had.

"Yes, the questions are thrilling but the answers are totally unconvincing."

But Fran had to admit that church affected him the same way. The questions of righteousness and salvation were exciting. But the answers the pastor and the Sunday School teacher provided were unconvincing. He realized with a start that in reality he was not even a Christian. To be a Christian was to believe. He did not believe. He felt sick. Were there no answers to the great questions of life? He was so desperate he actually considered reading the Bible. He had rarely done that. His church didn't encourage its members to read the Bible. The pastor spoon-fed verses out of context to the congregation to make a point. It had rarely convinced Fran.

"Should I read the Bible?" he mulled.

And in the dogged thoroughness instilled by his father and mother Fran decided he would start reading the Bible - right from its very beginning...

Chapter 2

The book of Genesis changed Fran's life.

The most obvious difference between Genesis and Greek philosophy was that the writer of Genesis did not postulate or hypothesize or rationalize but claimed to be relating historical fact. Genesis spoke with thundering authority. 'This is what happened,' gasped Fran. Yet he doubted. Could it be true? The great story overwhelmed him. All was created by God. The heavens and the earth were created by God. Nature was created by God. Man was created by God. God formed a special covenant with man. Yet man failed God from the very first generation. Then again and again. Every generation, it seemed, failed God. And men failed each other. They were flawed. When they exercised their own choices they failed.

"Yes," agreed Fran. "That is what mankind is really like. At last I'm finding answers - real answers - to the meaning of life!"

Yet, how could mankind be redeemed in God's eyes? Genesis was full of intriguing hints. Still in Chapter One God said, "Let us make man in our image." In *our* image? What could that mean? This was the Hebrew Bible. What could that plurality mean to a Hebrew? It was plain enough what the plurality meant to a Christian: the Trinity. It was no fluke because in Chapter Three God said, "Behold, the man is become as one of us, to know good and evil..." *Us?* What could it mean but the Trinity? And Chapter Three hinted at redemption. Speaking to the serpent God said that Eve's seed "shall bruise thy head." What could that mean but Christ's eventual triumph over the devil? Fran found Genesis a fountain of information. It seemed so true, so prophetic. Sometimes God let man muddle along without interfering. But sometimes God, apparently in exasperation, interfered, as He did with the Flood.

"God is intensely personal," concluded Fran.

Fran took to the Bible like a duck to water. Never had he thought so clearly. Immediately he seemed to grasp the enormous importance of chapters one through eleven of Genesis. These were the chapters - the so-called 'prologue' - before the arrival of Abraham. After Abraham came on the scene the Bible was clearly historical. But what of the prologue, the chapters before Abraham? Were chapters one through eleven the fumbling attempts of men ignorant

9

of science? Or were they a Jewish myth, of no more significance than any other ancient myth? Or were they intended originally as symbolism of great truths? Or were these opening chapters as historical as the rest of the Bible?

Fran pondered much on these opening chapters of Genesis, the so-called 'prologue'. Further reading convinced him the Jewish patriarchs regarded the prologue as historical. Adam was historical. The flood was historical. Noah was historical. Further reading convinced Fran the writers of the New Testament also regarded the prologue as historical. Paul quoted it several times. The writer of Hebrews quoted it. And most important of all: the most divine man in history regarded it as historical. Yes, in the book of Mark, Jesus quoted Genesis 1:27, then Genesis 2:24:

> But at the beginning of creation God 'made them male and female.' 'For this reason a man will leave his father and mother and be united to his wife, and the two will become one flesh.' So they are no longer two, but one. Therefore what God has joined together, let man not separate. (Mark 10:6-9)

Would Jesus have quoted what he believed to be a myth to make his argument? Of course not. Fran pondered the prologue. Finally he too decided it was historical. If not, then the prologue's thrilling explanation of God's purpose for mankind and mankind's disobedience were fictions. Fran had to give up on philosophies and the watered-down, liberal religion he had heard preached in his church. Now he devoured the rest of the Bible. He realized all the promises in the Old Testament were fulfilled in the New Testament. Within six months he was a Christian. But he faced a dilemma. As far as he knew he was a unique kind of Bible-believing Christian.

'Where are others like myself?' he wondered.

In the meantime the effect of his new outlook on his schoolwork was remarkable. At last he began to excel. He noted especially the clarity now of his writing in English class. It was a reflection of his clear thinking. He now had a foundation of truth under him. But he was also a senior, a senior who had prepared himself for vocational school. Still, he was performing so well now that his parents believed he could tackle nearby Drexel Institute after he graduated in June of 1930.

Drexel Institute was far more than a vocational school. It was established by financier Anthony Drexel in 1891 with great fanfare. Thomas Edison, U.S. Vice President Levi Morton and Andrew

Carnegie witnessed its beginning. It was innovative. For example it was only the third school in America to offer library science. By the time Fran decided to go there the school had four major divisions, one of which was Engineering. That was to be Fran's future. He would conquer the field his father would have conquered if he had not been forced to quit school at the age of 10.

Fran also had a brand new Model A Ford. His parents gave him the car for graduation. He was excited about his future and began to keep a diary for the first time. That summer of 1930 he took driving lessons, went to an art museum and began to become a regular visitor at the city library in Philadelphia. He became fascinated with Carl Sandburg, who wrote about common people in rough but alluring free verse. Fran found free verse an appealing form of expression. But Sandburg did not write just poetry. He also wrote a compelling biography of the younger Abraham Lincoln called *Prairie Years*. Sandburg's prose was almost Biblical in its curtness.

'And like the Bible Sandburg conveys the truth but leaves much unsaid,' Fran observed.

But Fran did not have the luxury of lazing around reading. He had to work, though summer jobs were scarce now. America was sliding into what would be called the 'Great Depression'. Fran found a few temporary jobs painting houses and he helped his father renovate their home on Ross Street. He also bought his first razor and a suit with long pants. Both were events that signaled manhood in those days. Before long pants boys wore knickers, pants that stopped just below the knees. But Fran was not happy. The fact that he had never found anyone who appreciated his unique kind of Christianity nagged at him. One sultry evening in August he strolled listlessly down Germantown Avenue. The horses of his youth were long gone. Now cars rattled up and down the street. On an empty lot on the corner of Ashmead Place someone had thrown up a large tent. It resounded with the singing of hymns.

"What on earth is going on in there?" blurted Fran.[1]

Fran eased inside the tent flap. He saw people sitting on rows of benches on each side of a center aisle. The floor was covered with sawdust. The people were indeed singing hymns, led by a man standing at a pulpit. Fran eased onto a bench near the back. The man at the pulpit began to preach. He spoke with an Italian accent but also with fire. And he preached from the Bible: verse after verse

---

[1] Schaeffer, *Tapestry*, 54.

but interspersed with the story of his own life. The preacher had redeemed himself from a life of crime through Christ! He had actually been in prison. Fran was enthralled. This preaching was so different from the boring sermons he had heard all his life. And when the preacher finished and invited people to come to the altar to commit themselves to Christ Fran almost leaped out of his seat.

The preacher asked him, "Young man, what are you here for, salvation or reconsecration?"[1]

The choice confused Fran. He did not know how to answer. Still, Fran was elated. He had publicly committed himself to Christ. And he had heard someone preach and reason from the Bible, in a common-sense way Fran had discovered for himself while reading. He found out the preacher was Anthony Zeoli and rushed home to write of his great discovery in his diary. But his entry that night contained far more than Anthony Zeoli. Fran wrote, "August 19, 1930 -Tent Meeting, Anthony Zeoli - have decided to give my whole life to Christ unconditionally."[2]

Fran's whole life to Christ unconditionally!

For over a year Fran had been obsessed with finding the meaning of life. Now he was convinced that living in Christ was the secret to finding truth. Yes, he was sure of it. On August 22 he returned to hear Zeoli. On August 26 he returned again, this time taking some of his friends. He was ecstatic but worried too. He no longer wanted to go to Drexel to study engineering. But he had no other plans. He couldn't be idle. So on September 2 he registered at Drexel for night school. He did not have the luxury of day school. He planned to work during the day to help pay for his education. Meanwhile he remained in turmoil. For the very next day he wrote in his diary that he had 'decided all truth is from the Bible'.[3] Could he allow himself to drift into a career that he really did not want to pursue? Although he did not respect the brand of preaching in his church he believed the churchmen were well-intentioned. He sought their counseling. First he talked to his Sunday School teacher. Then he talked to Sam Osborne, the Headmaster at Germantown Academy.

"Hampden-Sydney College," declared Osborne forcefully.

---

[1] Schaeffer, *Tapestry*, 55.
[2] Schaeffer, *Tapestry*, 55.
[3] Schaeffer, *Tapestry*, 56.

Fran knew nothing whatever about a college named Hampden-Sydney. But Osborne had gone there himself, so he told Fran about it with enthusiasm. Hampden-Sydney was a small but exclusive men's college in Virginia. In fact it was the tenth oldest college in America. Scotch-Irish Presbyterians had founded it in 1776. Students at the college actually fought the British at Williamsburg and Petersburg! Patrick Henry and James Madison were on the college's first Board of Trustees. Many of the people associated with the college went on to start other, now better-known, educational institutions like Union College in New York, Princeton Seminary and the University of Virginia. Hampden-Sydney would be a superb foundation for Fran's later seminary training, insisted Osborne.

"But I didn't even take a college preparation course in high school," murmured Fran dolefully.

Osborne had all the answers. After all, he was an educator. "You're only lacking the foreign languages. You can take courses at night in Latin and German at Central High school. You can start Hampden-Sydney the fall of 1931."

The fall of 1931! That was one year away. At Fran's age that seemed forever distant. So he agonized over Hampden-Sydney but began night school at Drexel on September 15. Only 10 days later he got a job at RCA Victor, the enormous electronics firm, for 32 cents an hour. The job was in New Jersey. Fran had to rise at 5:00 A.M., catch an early trolley car east to the Delaware River, and then cross on a ferry to Camden. After a full day of work at the RCA factory he grabbed supper at the nearby Horn and Hardart's Cafeteria, then he rushed back to Germantown and the Drexel Institute. After his evening of classes he returned home to study at the kitchen table!

His plan went haywire in October. At RCA Fran labored at a very menial job in a cavernous building full of conveyer belts. Feeding the parts onto the moving belts were men. Processing the electronic parts on the belts were women. Something happened that disturbed Fran very much. The foremen would promise a bonus for extra production - but only to the men. So the men poured more parts onto the belts and the women had to work harder and harder to keep up. But the women received nothing extra for this onslaught of work. The unfairness of it gnawed at Fran. The women were afraid to complain because jobs were so hard to find in 1930. Yet during one of these onslaughts one woman finally snapped.

"Strike!" she screamed.

Other women joined her. Yet some women objected to the strikers. Parts were scooting along the conveyer belts and crashing to the floor. Fights broke out among the women. It was too much for Fran. He found himself jumping onto a table.

"Yes! Strike! Strike!" he screamed.[1]

That was the end of his employment at RCA. He was the most expendable person in the entire building. But the next days seemed provident. He found a job near home driving a grocery truck. He was better off than he was before. His benefactor Sam Chestnut was a fellow church member. Fran's fellowship at the church was proving indispensable to his future. And it seemed every church member he talked to encouraged him to go into ministry, which in those days meant being a pastor. He now prayed with some of the members too. It felt very natural. By December he had to level with his parents.

"I'm thinking of quitting Drexler."

"But why?" asked his father. "Didn't you just get a B in your last Algebra test."

"It's not that, Pop. My grades are okay. It's just that I want to go to night school at Central High School so I can take courses in German and Latin."

Then Fran had to divulge the plan Sam Osborne, the headmaster at Germantown Academy, had suggested. When his father finally realized Fran was talking about becoming a minister he wilted. His feeling about the worthlessness of ministers went back to his earliest days. Not only did the ministers produce nothing in his opinion but they had an insufferable superior attitude. Besides, he felt betrayed. For years he had taught Fran to think mechanically and work with his hands. All that would be wasted. Ministers did nothing with their hands. Fran's mother did not voice objections but looked more despondent than Fran's father.

Fran's diary recorded the turmoil:

> December 14: Mother and dad still hostile to my plan. I hope guidance comes strongly and surely.
> December 15: Worried all day over mother and dad's not being back of me for my life's work. Decided to leave all to God.
> December 16: Talked to dad alone, he said to go ahead and that mother would get over it...[1]

---

[1] Schaeffer, *Tapestry*, 58.

The opposition had almost ended.

On the wall of his bedroom he put the Bible verse from the book of Joshua: "But as for me and my house, we will serve the Lord."

On January 30, 1931, his 19th birthday, he began his language studies at night at Central High School. His short stay at Drexel was over. How he found time to read for pleasure he could not say, but he read Grace Livingston Hill's *The Witness*. In the opening chapter of the novel a pious college student was teased mercilessly by other students. Oh Lord, was this to be Fran's destiny too? But in the novel one privileged student who casually watched the persecution eventually found redemption in Christ. But his salvation was not the end. It was the beginning. The student found himself serving others, tirelessly and with joy. Fran noted in his diary that *The Witness* shook him to the core.

By the fall of 1931 Fran was at last ready to go to Hampden-Sydney, thanks to providential hand that guided him as well as the friendship of an educator like Sam Osborne.

Fran packed his few belongings in a very sturdy wooden crate that he had painted porch-floor gray. He decided he would wear his suit. He didn't want to show up on campus in knickers. But he packed the knickers with the rest of his belongings: underwear, socks, shirts, gym clothes, raincoat, shaving brush, razor, towels, soap, toothbrush and a few books including his precious Bible. With that he was done. One thing he tried not to think about was how he would pay for his education. But now the difficulty - perhaps impossibility - hit him. A year at Hampden-Sydney cost $600. His father had said nothing yet. So in the back of his mind Fran expected he would have to find a job while he went to college. But at 30 cents an hour Fran could barely make $600 in one year of full-time working! So how would he be able to both work and study at such a high-powered college? This was not high school. Would Fran come back in a few weeks - thoroughly beaten? He just had to trust God.

The day he was to depart his father confronted him. It was 5:30 in the morning. "I don't want a son who is a minister, and I don't want you to go," he said with determination.[2]

Fran was stunned. He thought his father had softened. Since Fran began reading the Bible he had realized more and more what a

---

[1] Schaeffer, *Tapestry*, 59.

[2] Schaeffer, *Tapestry*, 60.

sin it was to oppose the wishes of parents. This blunt statement of opposition by his father hit him like a bolt of lightning. He reeled toward the door to the basement. He flung the door open and stumbled down the stairs. He had to pray. What should he do? He prayed for guidance. No answer came. He finally decided to cast lots. Many a churchman - even John Wesley - had done that before. 'Heads, I go to Hampden-Sydney' he told himself. He flipped the coin. It was heads. Still uncertain he flipped it a second time. Again it indicated he should go to Hampden-Sydney. He flipped the coin a third time. Yet again it indicated he should go. Surely he was meant to go. He trudged up the stairs. His father was still there.

"Pop, I've got to go. . . ."

Now his father looked like he had been struck by lightning. "I've got to go to work."[1]

Fran's father lurched toward the front door. Once outside he slammed it hard. Fan shuddered. Wasn't his father even going to say good-bye? Was he going to shut Fran out of his life forever? This farewell was a thousand times worse than Fran thought it would be.

But then he heard his father grunt outside the door, "I'll pay for the first half year."[2]

---

[1] Schaeffer, *Tapestry*, 62.
[2] Schaeffer, *Tapestry*, 62.

Chapter 3

A friend drove Fran to Hampden-Sydney in September 1931. The college was 300 miles southwest of Philadelphia over congested roads that crawled through Baltimore, Washington, D.C. and Richmond. After that urban stretch the campus of Hampden-Sydney seemed an oasis: beautiful, sprawling manicured lawns dotted with trees in early fall colors. However, the sight of young men in pressed white flannel pants, stylish blazers and brown-and-white saddle shoes slightly sickened Fran. The youths had expensive matched luggage too. They reeked of money. They also reeked confidence. Fran was unnerved by new social situations that now came with greater and greater frequency. He never failed now to pray for guidance.

His room assignment startled him too. "In Cushing Hall!"

Cushing Hall was the original building of the college. The red brick structure was box-like with tiers of shuttered windows. Entry was through a columned portico. Four-story high Cushing Hall was a superb example of Federal architecture. How had Fran rated such a splendid room assignment? Now he was excited. He thanked his friend for driving him to campus and hauled his gray crate inside the building.

He was shocked at what he saw inside the building. It was a 'no man's land'. A war zone. Holes were punched in the walls. Paint flaked off the walls. The deterioration only got worse as Fran wrestled his crate up the stairs. His room was on an upper floor. He was in 'Fourth Passage'. A huge upperclassman named Pat greeted him. Apparently Pat was the 'dorm counselor' for Fourth Passage. Pat didn't hide his amusement at Fran's gray crate.

"Who would you be, boy?" drawled Pat.

"Schaeffer."

"Where you from, boy?" drawled Pat.

"Philly."

"Well, you're a frosh now, boy. Worse than that you're a dink." He flipped a tiny cap to Fran. "Don't let me catch you outdoors without your dink cap."

Soon everyone was calling Fran 'Philly'. The odd fact was that all the inhabitants of Fourth Passage seemed unusually large - except five foot-six inch Fran. That fact was soon explained. This

17

Fourth Passage was the jock dormitory. Its inhabitants were as hard-nosed and ornery as they were athletic. Apparently some one thought putting a pre-ministerial student like Fran in their midst would be hilarious. It was possible, thought Fran, that the assignment had been made while he stood in line waiting for his room assignment. Someone may have decided he just didn't belong at Hampden-Sydney. What better way of getting rid of him than putting him in the very antithesis of holiness?

Within days Fran discovered the athletes who were not in their competitive season filled their time with heavy drinking. They had rifles in their rooms and many bullet holes penetrated the walls and floor boards. Their excuse for shooting was the eradication of a mouse or a bug. Fran's roommate Snerp was an upperclassman just as large as all the others, with one constant attitude toward Fran: surly. As a dink Fran had to attend to Snerp's wishes. If Snerp needed a light for his cigarette Fran had to find a match. If Fran moved too slow Snerp was allowed to swat Fran with a paddle. But Fran quickly learned Snerp preferred to strike with a coat hanger. There was a list of 'don'ts' that if violated allowed punishment of a dink. But Snerp made up violations too. He reminded Fran that he had little choice but to turn the other cheek. Fran seemed to have three strikes against him. Not only was Fran a Christian and from a working class background but he was also a Yankee. Students from the college had fought the Yankees during the Civil War. Students in residence during that war had officially been Company G of the 20th Virginia Regiment. Some of them seemed to be fighting the war yet. Snerp was one of them. Fran prayed he could endure such brutal behavior.

"Oh Lord, I'm being tested. Let me persevere."

Nevertheless Fran was not alone. There were many dinks on campus and they became united in their persecution. And that was actually the perverse justification for hazing. Besides comradery Fran had his Christianity to bolster him. He was sure Snerp could not push him to the breaking point. However, one day Pat was standing in the doorway chatting with Snerp. Fran was studying. Suddenly Fran's back exploded with pain. Snerp had whacked Fran for a phony reason - just to show off for Pat. Fran glared at the coat hanger in Snerp's hand. Snerp was so unjust that Fran snapped. He flew into the larger man. Fran had very strong arms and hands. Once he had a grasp on Snerp he was like a bulldog. They two careened around the room. Snerp stumbled and Fran flew on top of him. Quick as a cat Fran had Snerp in a merciless head lock. They two grunted and groaned as Fran squeezed and Snerp struggled to get loose.

Pat drawled, "You're the biggest little man I've ever seen, Philly."[1]

Pat made them break it up before Fran strangled Snerp. That was the last time Snerp took advantage of Fran. Fran didn't gloat over his 'victory'. From the standpoint of his Christianity he had failed. But he worshiped a forgiving God. So he repented, then tackled his studies and started a prayer group in the dormitory. Although the Student Christian Association had prayer meetings in the other dorms, there had not been one in Fourth Passage - until Fran volunteered to hold a weekly meeting. A few came, possibly out of curiosity about this feisty dink 'Philly'. Fran was shrewd enough to make the meeting very short. He read a few Bible verses, commented on them and then asked if anyone wanted to pray. Sometimes one or two would pray. Then Fran's prayer ended the meeting. So the prayer meeting became known as short and painless.

Although Fran had lost his self control with Snerp, other times he could show unbelievable patience and self control. An upper-classman nick-named 'Chisel' showed his anger at being asked to the prayer meeting by throwing a can of talcum powder at Fran. As blood trickled down Fran's face from a cut on his forehead he persisted with his invitation. Chisel had no remorse. He snorted that he would come to the meeting if Fran would carry him there.

"Let's go then," grunted Fran.

Fran threw the much larger man over his shoulder and lugged him to the meeting. Often Fran would get someone to join the group in exchange for a favor. Many times Fran helped drunken upper-classmen sober up. Often he put them to bed. It was not unusual now for a student to come into the dormitory stumbling drunk and scream for 'Philly'. He was always there. Not only did these sinners go to Fran's prayer meeting but often he persuaded them to go to church. It was amazing how meek they were during their 'hangover remorse'. College Church was not far from Cushing Hall. It con-formed to the Federal red brick architecture, with an enormous high pulpit in the sanctuary. The organ was in the balcony. Some students did not fail to remind Fran that Yankee troops had dam-

[1] Schaeffer, *Tapestry*, 121.

aged the left front door, implying the South had always taken the moral high road.

"Maybe I'll ask the residents of Five Points if they agree," he muttered to himself.

Since January 1932 when Fran struck up a friendship with a janitor named Johnny Morton he had walked every Sunday through the woods, then along cornfields to a small African-American community called 'Five Points'. There he taught Sunday School at Mercy Seat church to about ten children. Then Fran would visit Johnny Morton. Johnny's health was failing, so Fran would read the Bible and pray with him. In fact these visits didn't end even after Johnny died. Then Fran visited his grave at the churchyard.

Fran's first year on the campus of Hampden-Sydney was a non-stop whirlwind of activity. Fran had enormous energy and he never wasted a waking moment. He was elected to the Cabinet of the Student Christian Association and became a member of the Ministerial Association. Fran also began debating in the college's Literary Society. For exercise he did more than sober up upperclassmen. He ran the low hurdles for the track team. Some days he had so much energy he climbed the water tower.

Still he found time to read more than his college subjects. Once when he was not reading the Bible he read about 'Borden of Yale'. William Borden had been a rich, privileged young man who through Christ became selfless. He committed himself to evangelizing the Muslims, in China of all places. But while studying Arabic in Cairo he died from spinal meningitis at the age of 26. Borden did not realize his goal but remained a shining example of Christian service and selflessness. 'If only I could be like him,' prayed Fran. Always now he battled the self, often writing 'Not my will but thine'.[1] In fact he wrote down many of his spiritual thoughts:

> Cause and reason, love must be.
> But how shallow ours compared to that of Thee.
>
> A bug crossed a learned paper.
> Might not we too be crossing things
> We cannot read?

---

[1] Schaeffer, *Tapestry*, 124.

May I never be
too big
or too small.

Oh, God, not only for a time,
but for eternity may I serve thee.

Not only in the dim future of some eternal space, but right
here and now, may I know thee.

0 God, I thank Thee
for thy loving kindness to one who has sinned grievously
against Thee. Amen

0 God I thank Thee, that You use me to win souls for Thee.
0 give me strength to speak the words Thou wouldst have me
speak to them. Amen.

Fill my heart, 0 God.
With true love for thee, and the people you have made.
May I serve, but first I want to
learn to keep my eyes on Thee.
Amen.[1]

Fran wrote page after page of prayers.

As if Fran did not have enough to occupy his time, he also became a 'hasher' in the student cafeteria. This was a common way for
a student to defray expenses. For cleaning tables, serving food and
washing dishes the 'hasher' earned his meals. Like students everywhere the Hampden-Sydney boys soon complained of the tiresome
cafeteria menu. One night one of the students triggered a rebellion
by hurling his yams across the dining hall. Soon a 'food fight'
exploded. Fran was more than happy to take part. Instead of
humbly serving yams he was splattering them on a few smug
heads. When school authorities investigated the incident they
discovered - of course - that no one could remember who started it.

"A yam just plumb knocked it out of my memory," drawled one
wag who participated in the rebellion.

The cafeteria riot appeared spontaneous. But premeditated practical jokes were common at Hampden-Sydney, especially against

---

[1] Schaeffer, *Tapestry,* 125.

those perceived to be sanctimonious. One victim was Fran's Bible teacher Professor James Massey. The perpetrators of the joke had installed a cow in his classroom over the weekend. They had furnished the bovine plenty of fodder too. The cow had been there long enough to generate many 'cow pies'. Massey was of the stern school that one had to ignore such juvenile behavior. So his unfortunate students had to pick their way through the droppings and sit down as if nothing had happened. One hour later the students lurched from the classroom.

"Mercy!" they gasped.

Fran was only too happy to leave the stench too, although he usually relished the Bible class. Massey was just one of several professors who inspired Fran spiritually. Twyman Williams, the pastor of the college church, also inspired him, as did the college president Joseph Eggleston, who led the college as a real believer. Academically, Fran's most 'inspirational' professor was Maurice Allen, who taught philosophy. Allen loved a good argument. So did Fran at this time. The professor would invite Fran to his home where they sat around a potbellied stove and argued. Allen was much more liberal in his philosophy than Fran. It was a good thing they did not agree because the truly heated arguments honed Fran's skills at Christian 'apologetics', which meant 'defense' from its Greek root. It was Professor Allen who made Fran learn the rigors of logic and philosophy, so that he could not be dismissed as a lightweight in arguments with intellectuals. Fran quickly reached the point where no student could hold his own with him. He usually annihilated their arguments in a few minutes.

"Did you get the license number of that small truck from Philly that ran over me," cracked one of his victims.

For the first time Fran learned of the great upheaval within his own Presbyterian church. The renowned Princeton Seminary, once a bastion of conservative Presbyterian theology, had decided to embrace more liberal theologians. These theologians, influenced by the 'critical movement' in Germany, challenged every aspect of the Bible. The result of the challenge was to very effectively undermine every Christian belief. Suddenly the Bible became a book of myths written by well-intentioned but error-prone men. Suddenly the life of Christ was challenged. Because miracles were 'unnatural' they were stripped away. Soon Christ's divinity was stripped away. Finally the scholars of the critical movement decided that in all likelihood Christ never existed. He was simply an invention.

The conservative heavyweights at Princeton were appalled by the seminary's move in this same destructive direction. J. Gresham Machen, Cornelius Van Til and Robert Wilson left the Princeton Seminary, rather than be associated with such materialistic folly. They founded Westminster Theological Seminary. All this seemed providential for Fran, for he very much believed in the Bible. It had saved him. And the location of Westminster seemed just as providential.

"Philadelphia," he marveled.

Yes, Fran might even return home to go to Westminster Theological Seminary in Philadelphia. Fran now had high goals. In his first year he made the highest honor roll each term. There seemed no subject now that he did not excel at. He was very focussed. And yet he managed to also go occasionally into Farmville several miles away to see a movie. 'Talkies' were a very hot subject for students then. Talkies had only been around since 1927 but the technology was improving with lightning speed. And the available material, thousands upon thousands of plays and novels, seemed endless. The reservoir of actors and actresses also seemed limitless. America at that time had tens of thousands of amateurs and professionals acting on the stage. The sudden great quantity and high quality of talkies still seemed miraculous though. By 1932 the movie screens across America were already showing Clark Gable, Katherine Hepburn, Gary Cooper, Bette Davis, James Cagney, Barbara Stanwyck, Ronald Colman, Joan Crawford, Spencer Tracy, Bing Crosby, Humphrey Bogart and John Wayne - virtually all the stars who would dominate the screen for many years to come.

Fran also occasionally dated girls from a teacher's college at Farmville. But he was far too serious for most of them. And even the ones who were serious did not enjoy talking about the kinds of things Fran wanted to talk about. With the exception of the ministerial students this was also true of Hampden-Sydney students. But by the end of his first year he was accepted by one and all at his college. He had proved he could take it and dish it out too. And he was a 'good sport', running on the track team and helping drunks to their beds. In June 1932 he returned to his home in Germantown after a very successful freshman year.

"'We are very much pleased with your boy's conduct and excellent work'[1] is what the dean of your college wrote us," said Pop proudly when Fran returned.

Naturally Fran went to his church as soon as possible. His Sunday School teacher and Sam Osborne, the Headmaster at Germantown Academy, wanted to know all about his first year. He had certainly done credit to them. On the night of June 26 he attended the Young People's Meeting at his church.[2] He sat next to an old friend named Dick. The title of the talk that night was 'How I know that Jesus is not the Son of God, and how I know that the Bible is not the Word of God'! Fran was astonished. Did Fran's church show no discernment? Why not invite the devil to speak? Suddenly Fran realized that the liberalization of the Princeton Seminary was just the tip of the iceberg. Liberalization was taking place within the Presbyterian church itself. What was once denounced as heresy was now tolerated as thought-provoking scholarship. He sat and listened to what seemed like simple-minded blasphemy from the young speaker named Ed, all the while jotting down Ed's logic. He was angry as he realized he could not fend off all the points Ed was making. But Fran was on his feet as soon as Ed finished his talk.

"You all may think what I am going to say is influenced by my having sat all this year under a Bible teacher at Hampden-Sydney College whom you would term 'old-fashioned.' He has taught the Bible to be the Word of God, and I do believe that too. I want to say that I know Jesus is the Son of God, and He is also my Savior, and has changed my life. I've been away all year, and this is the first time any of you has seen me since college, but although I can't answer all the things Ed has said, I want you to know just where I stand."

After Fran finished his 'defense', a tiny, dark-haired girl stood up to speak. She appeared to be about 18. Fran nearly fall off his chair as she countered the speaker's arguments very effectively with quotes from J. Gresham Machen and Dick Wilson, two of the Presbyterian church's powerhouse theologians. Her arguments were organized and flowed logically. She was brilliant. The tiny girl had done what Fran had wanted to do but had not been able to do!

---

[1] Schaeffer, *Tapestry*, 127.

[2] Account of the first meeting between Fran and Edith in Schaeffer, *Tapestry*, 131-132.

Fran whispered to his friend, "Who on earth is that girl? I didn't know anyone in this church knew that kind of thing."

"That is Edith Seville, and she has just moved here from Toronto, Canada. Her parents used to be missionaries in China."

"Will you introduce me to her?"

Fran could think of nothing else the rest of the meeting. After the last hymn was sung and the benediction delivered, Fran had to restrain himself from hurdling chairs to get to the tiny girl. He and his friend Dick had to wiggle through the crowd. Would she disappear in the meantime? He felt like he was hyperventilating. Never had he so wanted to meet a girl! But suddenly there she was, tiny and very proper. She had a sharp straight nose, square jaw and tiny mouth. She was not a classic beauty but she was very attractive.

Fran's friend Dick said, "Edith, I want to introduce you to Fran Schaeffer. Fran, this is Edith Seville."

The tiny girl looked at Fran and smiled. Her smile was straight and brilliant. Shaken, Fran blurted, "May I take you home?"

"I'm sorry, but I already have a date."

"Break it," said Fran aggressively.

"Well . . . yes, I guess I will."

Fran was unhinged. Immediately he felt rotten for coercing her into breaking a date. So he was relieved to find out Edith's 'date' was to go to her girl friend Ellie's house. Others from the meeting, including Dick, were going to go there too. So Fran said he would drive Edith to Ellie's house in his Model A. He invited Dick and Ellie to ride too. On the way to his car Fran fumbled around for his car key in obvious panic, much to the amusement of Ellie and Dick. He was completely discombobulated by the tiny articulate girl. She seemed a miracle. And as he learned more about 17-year-old Edith Seville the miracle was confirmed...

Chapter 4

"I was born Edith Rachel Seville the morning of November 3, 1914, at Flower Garden Lane in the Chinese town of Wenchow," said Fran's new friend.

In the Chekiang Province, Wenchow was a sizeable river port 200 miles south of the giant seaport city of Shanghai. Edith's parents were missionaries for the China Inland Mission who first met in China. Edith's mother Jessie Greene had gone there in 1899, her father George Seville in 1902. In fact Jessie had survived the bloody Boxer Rebellion of 1899. The Chinese Empress had tried to bolster her sagging popularity by blaming all China's problems on foreigners. In the process she loosed thugs called 'boxers' all over China to terrorize foreigners. The boxers murdered hundreds of missionaries. The China Inland Mission, which had 200 missions throughout China, lost 58 missionaries and 21 children. So Jessie had endured a test of fire, and China remained a powder keg.

"The China Inland Mission was founded by the Englishman Hudson Taylor in 1865," continued Edith.

Taylor insisted his missionaries live and dress Chinese. The greatest stumbling block to missionary work - besides the ever present physical dangers - was learning the language and its severely different dialects. For the truth was that the Chinese from Canton could not understand the Chinese from Beijing. The customs were similar, the written language was the same, yet the spoken language was different!

"On March 29, 1905, several years after an uneasy peace was declared, George Seville married Jessie Greene," Edith informed Fran.

The Sevilles lived within the missionary compound in Wenchow. Janet Elizabeth was born in 1906. In 1907, John was born but died at only eight months. Elsa Ruth was born in 1909. By the time Edith was born in 1914 Janet was a rambunctious eight-year-old away at boarding school. Mother Jessie taught at the mission's girls school so when baby Edith looked out of her bamboo playpen, called a 'gatse', she saw her five-year-old sister Elsa and her Chinese nursemaid or 'Amah'. But because Elsa left for boarding school only a year later Edith was left alone with her Amah.

"I became as Chinese as I was American," said Edith.

China was a country of great mistrust. Every city was walled. Many things *within* a city were walled. The many buildings of the mission compound were on a large tract of land surrounded by a wall. Next to the two-story missionary house, which was surrounded by a pleasant verandah, was a garden of grass and bamboo trees. The Chinese students of the mission school lived in dormitories. The boys and girls went to separate schools. Services at the mission church were not only for those in residence but any in Wenchow who wanted to attend. Also in the compound were houses for the Chinese pastor, the cook and many other Chinese who worked there. One of these houses belonged to the gatekeeper. He would peer through small latticed windows to see who might enter the great locked doors.

But inside the walls Edith danced and sang with joy. She especially liked to twirl so hard her little smock would billow out like a tent. Her favorite song was:

> Fly little bug!
> Fly little bug!
> Little bug, fly away where?
> Fly away to Amah's nose![1]

As she sang the last line Edith's little hand fluttered out to touch Amah's nose. But of course Edith sang the song in Chinese. Edith was not supposed to eat Chinese food very often - things like pork balls, banana fritters, zingdaw syrup, and buffalo cream were much too rich, her parents insisted - but Amah had a mind of her own. She and Edith made a habit of visiting Chinese friends at meal times. Their hosts happily taught Edith to use chopsticks and perform such dining techniques as eating rice and drinking tea at the same time without mixing the two! Amah and the cook loved to take Edith to market where they taught the bright-eyed tot to forcefully haggle over the prices of fish and eggs. 'I can't pay that much for those very bad onions!' Edith would chirp in Chinese. The Chinese adored little Edith, dubbing her Mei Fuh for 'beautiful happiness' and spoiling her into a very willful child.

'Fichaw!' barked tiny Mei Fuh, a very impolite word for telling someone to shut up.

But morning and evening her parents influenced her too. So she began collaring any available Chinese children - usually her

---

[1] Edith Schaeffer, *Meih Fuh*. (Boston: Houghton Mifflin, 1998), 43.

playmates - to preach to them. 'Do you want to preach to me?' she would ask politely, but in a split second she would blurt, 'No? Then I will preach to you!' Although she was not afraid to question her parents about Bible stories she tore into any of her listeners who dared question them. She was a fierce little evangelist.

"I was going to get those stubborn playmates of mine into heaven if I had to harangue them all day," Edith told Fran, laughing.

One morning Edith encountered the director of the mission taking a walk. Bold, she just assumed she could join him. But he cautioned her that he was praying. And what prayer! Each day, he told her, he started by praying for four hours. Four hours! That seemed like forever to Edith. The director prayed for the mission and everyone who lived there. He kept a list of names in his palm, which he would refer to. But all he needed was the reminder. After he read the next name, he knew enough about that person to know what concerns to voice. Edith was impressed by his caring and by the fact he did not tell God what must be done.

"He had total confidence God was listening to him," said Edith, remembering.

When Janet and Elsa returned from school on breaks they read to Edith and taught her games. Once Elsa read *Pilgrim's Progress* to her. John Bunyan's great classic was an allegory about a man seeking salvation. Then they played 'Pilgrim's Progress'. Tiny Edith had to sling a pillowcase stuffed with things over her back. That of course was Bunyan's 'Burden of sin'. Then Edith had to struggle through the quagmire called 'Slough of Despond', eventually finding her way to the Wicket Gate, guarded by a gatekeeper.

'Who goes there?' boomed the gatekeeper, Elsa.

Edith shouted, 'I am a poor burdened sinner...'

'Enter!' answered Elsa, yanking tiny Edith through the imaginary gate so the devil could not get one last arrow into her. 'Look before you!' yelled Elsa. 'Do you see the narrow Way? It was prepared by the Patriarchs, Prophets, Christ and his Apostles. It is the way you must go!'

By following the 'Way', which was between two walls called Salvation, Edith eventually labored up a stairway to a Cross. At that point she bowed to the cross and let the pillowcase slide off and bump down the stairs.

'He has given me rest by his sorrow, and life by his death!' she screamed with joy.

Free of guilt! Saved! And it felt so good to have the burden off her back. Edith loved the game. She knew she was naughty. What a relief to know Jesus offered forgiveness to anyone who would confess and ask for forgiveness. One did not have to live with guilt! And even more, Jesus offered salvation and eternal life.

"My life wasn't all fun and games," Edith said to Fran, changing moods.

One memory of those childhood days before the age of five was particularly vivid. Edith was diagnosed with the dread disease trachoma, a bacterial infection of the eyes spread by flies. It would be years later that she would learn trachoma in those days was considered a certainty to cause permanent blindness. But Dr. Stedeford, the Methodist missionary doctor who had delivered her, was a Godsend. He knew of a very radical procedure that might remove the infection. He squeezed little Edith's head between his knees, rolled back her eyelids and pumiced the crusty infection off her lids and eyes!

"It was an experience one never forgets," gulped Edith.

Yet she fully recovered. After that though, Edith had another painful experience. She tipped over a pail of boiling water that Amah was going to pour for a bath. The water scalded both Edith's legs. For days she was in pain. But once again her superb doctor prevented permanent damage. Her Chinese friends did everything possible to distract her from her pain. They gave her two white rabbits and a baby goat. Edith was crazy about the goat. It was so gentle and friendly. As her legs healed she manhandled the tiny, uncomplaining animal more and more. But a day came when she decided she would butt heads with her growing goat. Two budding horns left two black and blue welts on her forehead.

"After that uneven contest my little goat was allowed to join the older goats."

Edith was spoiled but she began to understand that not everyone would treat her kindly. The Chinese in the compound introduced her to their very sophisticated art of flying kites. Their kites were magnificent box-shaped structures. Once, with the help of the gatekeeper and a kitchen boy, she had her lovely box kite flying high above the garden. Edith was thrilled. Suddenly she noticed another kite veering toward hers. It tangled with her kite and before she could react the string was yanked from her hand. Bawling, she watched the two kites disappear beyond the tops of the compound buildings. Apparently the operator of the other kite was beyond the compound wall.

'A kite thief,' muttered the gatekeeper.

How cruel! But one day came when she realized deeper evil than that lurked in mankind. Her mother was with her in a rickshaw, a two-wheeled carriage pulled not by a horse but a man. They were going to go across town so Edith could visit her playmate Nina. The man pulling the rickshaw had built up speed on the cobblestone streets so that he was running in full stride. Suddenly a toddler appeared ahead of them. The man pulling the rickshaw deftly kicked the child aside! Edith became hysterical. Was the baby all right? To her horror they careened ahead - without stopping. Her mother assured her the child was all right. Edith did not believe her. How could they know for sure?

"And soon I realized I would never know," said Edith sadly to Fran.

The enormity of evil outside the compound where she lived only grew with her increasing awareness. Once when her Amah walked with her in the streets they passed a pagoda near the great city wall of Wenchow. Edith heard babies crying. 'Where are they?' chirped Edith. What little girl doesn't love babies? Amah looked stricken. Finally she had to tell Edith the truth. That particular pagoda at the wall was where people left their unwanted girl babies. The babies were simply left outside the wall to die. The crying Edith heard was a symphony of death! Now she listened more acutely. Not all the babies were crying lustily. Some were whimpering, in their last weak attempts to summon help.

'But why?' cried Edith.

'Many Chinese feel only sons bring the family honor. Why raise a worthless girl?' Then Amah was quick to add, 'That is why your parents came here. These people don't know any better. Soon they will all know about Jesus and the killing will stop.'

Did no one else feel the evil around them like Edith? The more she dwelt on the girl babies the more horrified she became. After all, was she not a girl? After that when she watched a Chinese parade she despised the leering masks of their gods, some on grotesque figures on stilts, some on slithering dragons. She began to realize this was the idol worship the God of her Bible condemned. This was the kind of devilish worship that allows babies to be thrown away. Because if the worship had been directed at the living God, the killing of babies would have been unimaginable.

"So at that point I was not unhappy to learn my family was going back to America for a while," Edith told Fran.

She had heard many wonderful things about that birth place of her parents. Besides, her father said it was only a visit for perhaps up to a year. Then they would be reassigned to China for another seven years. So Edith's good-byes were tearful but only the good-byes of someone going on vacation. And in no time at all they were on a ship sailing from Shanghai to the west coast of America. It was the summer of 1919.

"I wasn't quite five years old," said Edith.

The voyage lasted one month. Edith had a wonderful time running the long decks of the ship. The church services seemed especially lively with raucous hymn-singing. Edith was even allowed to pick her favorites. Then she sang at the top of her lungs. She was very spoiled. Once she and a playmate sneaked into a cabin and ate chocolates from a box. But mother Jessie found out and angrily told Edith she had to go back on her own to the owner of the chocolates and confess. This was no longer a game like 'Pilgrim's Progress'. Edith really did feel guilty. Her heart was hammering as she went back to the cabin. Her face burned with shame as she confessed.

The owner, a pleasant woman, blunted the apology. 'Oh, child, I should have offered you some chocolates long ago.'

After they reached the United States they settled in Germantown. Edith's parents would work at the China Inland Mission headquarters at West School Lane. Edith began kindergarten that fall at the Stevens' School for Girls in the Chestnut Hill area. Her days as the pampered little princess were over until she could return to China. But after one year the Seville family learned they would never be returning to China. Mother's health would not allow it. She was 45 years old and had served 20 years in China already.

"So for two years we lived in California," Edith told Fran.

Edith experienced the extreme prejudice there against Asians. In fact her bigoted schoolmates regarded her as Chinese! Edith fought back, learning how futile one felt against backward bigots. But this period was also an onslaught of childhood diseases. She seemed to be in bed as often as she was in school. It was Elsa more than anyone else who entertained her during these illnesses. For one year Edith's father left to go to school in Boston, so he could enter the Presbyterian ministry. During his absence Grandfather Merritt came to live with his daughter Jessie and her three daughters.

"He was in his eighties but no idler," said Edith fondly. "He still painted houses."

While father George was gone the family attended the Baptist church. Mother had been a Baptist before she joined the nondenominational China Inland Mission. Because Edith had not been immersed in her baptism she could not take communion. Communion was very important to her. Edith suddenly found herself meeting the board of deacons and being quizzed on her beliefs. With her missionary background her answers were very sophisticated for a seven-year-old. Soon she had been immersed and she was taking communion. But within the year she and her family moved to New Wilmington, Pennsylvania, where father was being started in the Presbyterian ministry. Later they moved to Newburgh, New York, where her father was pastor of the Westminster Independent Presbyterian Church.

"I was eight and Newburgh was my fourth school in three years!" said Edith.

But life at Newburgh, a small town on the Hudson River closer to New York City than Albany, proved stable. Both Janet and Elsa were able to graduate high school there. However, Edith's father's salary was so meager the family constantly practiced economies. Meals were simple but inventive. All Edith's clothes were homemade. Fortunately her mother became a very skilled seamstress. Edith's clothes actually seemed more stylish than the store-bought clothes of her classmates. Mother's ingenuity inspired Edith. Her genuine love of homemaking would never leave her. She herself tried to make extra money by cooking and selling candy. Every dollar looked very large to her. But she really settled in and became American at Newburgh. China seemed longer and longer ago. Edith belonged to the Girl Scouts, took gymnastics at the "Y" and learned to swim at the "Y" camp. In school she excelled at mathematics, English and the sciences. She disappointed her father in only one respect.

'Edith, you have no aptitude at all for Latin,' he complained.

Edith's best friend was Emily. Emily was a Christian Scientist, so the two girls had many lively debates. The discussions were basic philosophy. To Emily matter did not really exist. 'Mind is all and all is mind,' she insisted.[1] Of course Edith did not agree. She was well versed in fundamental arguments. She also understood the modern-

---

[1] Schaeffer, *Tapestry*, 141.

ism movement afflicting the mainline Protestant churches, especially Presbyterians. Her parents were very conservative. They discouraged the sins of 'worldliness', like dancing, playing cards, smoking, drinking alcohol and even going to see movies. Alcohol her parents especially fought. America had started prohibition of alcohol in 1919. But by the middle 1920's the prohibition was failing. People broke the law everywhere. Many liberals called for a repeal of the law.

'Everybody's drinking anyway,' they railed, 'so why not make it legal?'

Church women fought this repeal. Many belonged to the Women's Christian Temperance Union, wearing white ribbons on their dresses that symbolized purity. Edith went to a meeting of the WCTU once and was amazed as the members chanted pledges, and then shouted, 'White ribbon! White ribbon!' This kind of group frenzy frightened her. Yet she agreed with the women. Alcohol was the nation's prime home-wrecker.

Edith's mother was usually far too busy to get very active in such protest movements. Church had morning and evening services on Sunday, as well as a Wednesday evening prayer meeting. And there were many pastoring and social activities. In addition, funds had to be constantly raised with church bizarres.

"Although my parents would much prefer tithing," Edith admitted to Fran.

Just when Edith was ready to begin her sophomore year in high school she learned two very significant things, one of which really stunned her...

Chapter 5

"One rare evening in our Newburgh home I was truly alone with my mother," Edith told Fran.

Just out of the blue Edith's mother told her she had been married before! Edith was thunderstruck. Married before? Yes, Jessie Merritt worked as an accountant when she met Walter Greene. Walter was a committed Christian who wanted to go to China. After they fell in love China became their common goal. They saved their money so they could go to Toronto Bible College where they would be trained for China. They married in 1894. Soon Jessie was carrying a child. But within one year her marriage was ashes. Not only had her son been born dead but three weeks later feverish Walter was diagnosed with terminal 'galloping consumption'. It just seemed days later that Walter died.

Jessie remembered his deathbed numbly, 'He looked handsome, but too bright - like a lamp that flares up just before it burns out.'[1]

'Oh, mother,' cried Edith.

At only 21 Jessie was a widow who also mourned for a dead son. How could anyone bear such sadness? No wonder mother had never talked about it. Such unbearable tragedies. Memories like that made the news that the Sevilles were going to move again seem very minor indeed. Just before Edith's sophomore year the Sevilles moved to Toronto, Canada, where her father worked as Assistant Editor of China Inland Mission's monthly magazine *China's Millions*. Edith's social life had been so restricted she did not miss anyone in Newburgh except Emily.

She would have been bright but invisible in her new high school in Toronto, but she distinguished herself by being argumentative. One could not ignore her very long because the tiny girl spoke up in classes defending Christian principles. While other students blithely accepted any unsupported notion they heard about evolution she fought it fiercely. To her the theory of evolution required far more blind faith than belief in God. She knew in particular that her fellow students knew nothing about fossils or biological taxonomy, yet they accepted every so-called 'fact' blindly. She was certain the teachers were not much more knowledgeable than the students.

---

[1] Schaeffer, *Tapestry*, 87.

"I wasn't entirely an outspoken 'troublemaker' with no social life," Edith told Fran.

She was allowed to go to sporting events. Even as zealous as she was for her beliefs she began to deceive her parents. Often she went to parties after the football, basketball or hockey game. She told her parents she only played games there but in fact she was dancing. Finally she also began to sneak off to go to movies. By 1930 movies were very hot. Who didn't want to see the talkies everyone talked about? And yet she felt like a phony, like she was play-acting. No one other than her parents ever talked about anything serious.

'You really don't know me, because I'm not really being me,' she would say to her date.

'Really?' the boy would say, expecting a joke.

'I'm really a very serious person, and I intend to spend my life making truth known.'

'That's weird,' the boy would say, showing his disappointment.[1]

She felt like a phony with 'normal' kids and there seemed to be no Christian youth groups where her family was living. Reading became her great escape and pleasure. She read of other periods of history, and of great personalities. They became as real to her as the people she met in school. The great people in the books were so much more interesting too. She began to realize reading was in one sense reality. It opened the door to the reality of the past. Still, not all her reading was about giants of the past. She devoured the wonderful books of Lucy Maud Montgomery: *Ann of Avonlea, Ann of Green Gables, Ann of the Island, Emily of New Moon* and others. She felt like she had actually lived on Prince Edward Island herself.

"It seemed the very trees and meadows, the shoreline and special rocks were part of my own life," she told Fran.

Yet sometimes Edith daydreamed not of living the sweet rural life of Prince Edward Island nor of living the life of service in a mission in China - but of living the life of an art student in Paris. In her daydream she took a homely sky-lighted 'garret' and transformed it into a tasteful, comfortable paradise. She prepared gourmet meals with nothing more one pot on a small flame. She sewed, cooked and decorated. She was ingenious at homemaking like her mother. Yet what a peculiar daydream, for art scarcely entered into it. The dream was all about her miraculous skills

---

[1] conversation from Schaeffer, *Tapestry*, 115.

creating a homey environment where two or twelve could gather to eat, sleep, talk, read or pray in the most pleasant atmosphere.

"Just before my senior year at the Toronto high school my father was transferred to Germantown," sighed Edith, "because the office of *China's Millions* was moving there."

Her third high school! Well, she was a senior. Surely there could not be a fourth! The family found a suitable house on Ashmead Place South, just off Germantown Avenue. The home was pleasant with a brick fireplace and bay windows. Edith Seville was only 16, young for a high school senior. She was unknown to her classmates, even though a dozen years before she had lived in Germantown to attend Stevens' School for Girls. She was tiny. She had a peculiar accent. She was contrary in class. She was very restricted on what she was allowed to do socially - unless she deceived her parents.

Although Edith occasionally bent the rules she also tried to be Godly. One of her greatest shocks was to discover her older sister Janet no longer believed in God! College destroyed Janet's faith. The Bible now embarrassed Janet. Rational people, she insisted, simply did not believe such fairy tales. Edith was horrified. How does one bring a person like Janet back in the fold? Not with pleading. Only rational arguments would work. So Edith became more of a bookworm than ever. She had heard discussions on 'modernism' and such all her life. But now she avidly read J. Gresham Machen and other conservative Presbyterian theologians. She took notes. She marshaled her arguments. She inspected all religious books for signs of modernism. She even went into Philadelphia to hear J. Gresham Machen and Dick Wilson defend the faith at the Westminster Seminary. In the back of her mind was the fear that she might lose her own faith. College was not that far off for her.

Edith spent a forgettable senior year at Germantown high School. The tiny difficult girl with the funny accent graduated in May 1932. Beyond that her parents encouraged her to go on with her education at nearby Beaver College, which had become associated with the Presbyterian church. She really did intend to spend her life making the truth known. But as yet she was not sure how she would do that.

"Then in June 1932 I met an equally difficult, outspoken person named Francis Schaeffer...," laughed Edith.

Fran and Edith overwhelmed each other. He was 20 years old, she 17. For several years each had sought some companion of the opposite sex to talk to about the burning truth of Christianity. And if they had never developed a physical love for each other they would surely have developed *agape:* Christian love. For the two seemed in perfect spiritual harmony from the beginning.

When Fran first called on Edith he was delighted to notice how near her family's house on South Ashmead Place was to the lot where he had walked into Anthony Zeoli's revival tent not quite two years before. Edith seemed more providential than ever. Fran was well received by Edith's family. After all, he was a pre-ministerial student who might be wooing a minister's daughter. From that moment of encouragement from her family he could not imagine life without Edith. But he did not tell Edith, so she was not quite as sure. In those days when men usually made all the advances, how could a proper woman be sure about anything?

Fran took a job selling hosiery door to door. Would he become too busy to see Edith? No, he did not let a day go by without seeing Edith or writing her a letter if he or she was out of town. When the Sevilles left for a two-week vacation in missionary cottages near Atlantic City, Fran wrote his first letter to Edith. As a result he was invited to spend the next weekend there with them. Enchanted with each other Fran and Edith walked the entire seven miles of the boardwalk barely noticed the crashing waves beside them. They spoke of things they had never been able to discuss with anyone their own age before.

'And we never to run out of things to talk about,' reflected Fran.

Fran's diary became swollen with things he had done with Edith. They enjoyed concerts at the outdoor amphitheater Robin Hood Dell. They attended concerts indoors too. At one concert at the Academy of Music they were shocked. At the conclusion the conductor Stokowski had stooges in the audience stand up and sing the Communist anthem! The enemy was everywhere. Fran and Edith discussed the conservative Presbyterian J. Gresham Machen's *Christianity and Liberalism*. They slipped off to see the Greta Garbo movie 'As You Desire Me'. Greta played a woman with amnesia, suddenly confronted with being a wife to a husband who was a stranger. The premise, mildly shocking for the day, led to no satisfying outcome in the movie.

Often Fran would spend the day with the Sevilles, playing tennis with George Seville. Both men were short, wiry and very competitive. Whereas Fran ran track in college, George had played football and tennis. George was 56 years old. He had spent his first 12 years on an orchard farm near Pittsburgh. But as a youth he had excelled

37

at languages - hence his disappointment that Edith did so poorly with Latin. But Fran learned that George loved to have fun as a youth. Even when he was doing well as a student he was often in hot water for breaking rules. He was not only an athlete but played a guitar. Moreover he loved to mimic! Sometimes it seemed to Fran that he was the more serious of the two. It was not a case of a girl friend with a stern father but a case of a girl friend with a stern suitor. For Fran was a suitor, even if Edith did not know it yet.

'But she soon will know,' he promised.

He procrastinated until the time neared for him to return to Hampden-Sydney. Then he took her for an evening ride in his car. He parked by a shimmering river. The moon was full. He kissed her. But then he felt guilty at the onrush of hot thoughts.

"I'm sorry. I shouldn't have done that..." he stammered.

Edith was disappointed. Of course he should have done that! And why did he stop so abruptly? Was there something wrong with her? She felt anger. She became sarcastic. Only later did she realize Fran had done the right thing.

That night he wrote in his diary: It would be an easy matter, to let my passions run riot. Easy that is, if it were not for Thee, guiding us, keeping us strong. May we find our happiness in Thy way.[1]

Us. We. Yet Fran left for college, not having told Edith of his intentions to marry her. He didn't doubt that if God's plan was for him to marry Edith it would most certainly happen. He trusted God completely. Somehow it didn't occur to him that Edith might be in agony wondering how much he cared for her. Fran didn't realize what an advantage he had over Edith in many ways. Whereas he went back to Hampden-Sydney to completely immerse himself in college, Edith just dipped her toe in college. Her family did not have the money to let her live on campus. She commuted. She took the trolley along Germantown Avenue to Wayne Junction. From there she rode a train to the college campus in Jenkintown. She had abandoned her dream of studying art in Paris but not the dream of creating a home. Her major was Home Economics, a course of study that led to a Bachelor of Science degree. It was a difficult and peculiar degree with four years of chemistry combined with foods, dietetics, dressmaking, interior decorating and art appreciation!

'Perfect curriculum for marriage,' reflected Edith, quite pleased with her choice of a major. For she was as trusting as Fran. Surely

---

[1] Schaeffer, *Tapestry*, 135.

they would marry. It was God's plan. Had two people ever been more compatible, more right for each other?

They flooded each other with letters. Twice a week at first. But that was not enough. Soon it was three times. Finally it was every day, including Sunday. In those days Sunday delivery was possible for extra postage. Their love for each other flowered in the letters. Then when Fran returned to Germantown on Christmas break their relationship took a setback. Fran was frightened at the intensity of the desire he felt for her. Finally on the afternoon of December 31 he was totally confused.

"We're too fond of each other ," he blurted to her. "I'll only have to leave you behind. Where I'm going no woman can follow..."

Edith couldn't believe her ears. She was numb as they mumbled good wishes to each other and parted. One moment she thought she was going to marry Fran. The next moment they were parted forever! By dinner she was sobbing into her tomato soup. Mother tried to comfort her. Her father complained that once again he was in the dark. In that case dark turned out to be best because after dinner the phone rang. It was Fran.

"I've been so miserable since I left you. I know now I can't live without you. Please can I come down for a half hour?"

Forever had lasted two hours!

Fran came and talked breathlessly. He pleaded with Edith to wait for him until he finished college. There it was. At last, a proposal! New Year Eve 1932. He finished his proposal with a kiss. After Fran returned to college in Virginia their letters flowed daily again. Still, letters were not enough. Edith advanced the idea each should read the church devotional *Daily Light* at exactly the same time each day. That way they were bonded in time, though apart. Fran thought it was a great idea. But the letters, though delayed, bonded their direct thoughts. One of Edith's 1933 letters soothes Fran's sense of failure over doing something wrong, then being chastised by other students for 'not practicing what he preached'.

> Franz dear -
>
> We humans fall so far short of our ideals at times that it is discouraging. But we wouldn't want to preach that side of it - I mean we wouldn't want to say - "Well, once a month it's a fine thing to break through and do something entirely opposite to what you believe is right" - just because all of us do do things like that. We don't want to sanction it - just for the sake of preaching what you practice! We want to really

preach the Christian life - and then we want to live it so far as is possible but because we are human - we can't be perfect. That's where forgiveness comes into the picture - forgiveness for our mistakes. I don't know whether you can read into this what I am trying to say or not. Anyway - I think the fellows are all wrong in picking on one small slip - when there is so much in your life that is parallel to your "preaching." In fact I think it might help your influence for them to know that a Christian is just as human as anyone else - the difference is that he has someone to go to with his mistakes - and difficulties - to get them smoothed out - and that instead of pulling him down . . . he goes on again - a bit more prayerfully - and a bit stronger for having found his feet and climbed up the hill he slid down. See??? That's what I think anyway. And - furthermore I think you're splendid - I know it and I admire the way you straightened it out. I admire your courage to do it immediately, and I love you all the more...

... I've just been listening - with one ear - to a conference in protest of Hitler's treatment of the Jews...

Sweet dreams . . .

Ede[1]

Another letter in early 1933 read:

Franz -

Every word of your letter struck a responsive chord in me - it was so marvelously alive - not just words. Since then I have had feelings - emotions I never knew I possessed - I don't know how to describe it . . . but I've wanted to weep - that sounds contradictory - but it's true. . . It's not just love, it is bigger than that ...

Other people will know "the wonderful man of God" - "the splendid person" - the "peach of a guy" - but I will be the only one who will know him perfectly - at all times -and be his companion - through everything! Why Franz, it seems such a perfect life to be going to live when I have done nothing to deserve it - that all I can say is - "God is good to allow it," perhaps even to plan it - life is short - but there is an eternity ahead of that, and to think that through it all - you will be there Young man, have you any faults? I think, "Now eve-

---

1 Schaeffer, *Tapestry*, 145-6.

ryone has faults - what are Franz's" - and I say now - "forget that you love him - look at it impersonally" but no matter how much I pucker my brow nary a one can I conjure up - It wouldn't make any difference if you did have - but you don't. Being late - or running the car into sand doesn't count - they are virtues that make life interesting! - an adventure you know!

...There is a new moon a tiny sliver of a moon - have you seen it yet? . . . I think I'd better end here - I want to do some reading an English play if I can find it on our shelves. I'll try to write a note in the middle of the week-but I promise you a fat one when exams are over!!

Ede[1]

Page nine of her promised 'fat one' read:

. . . It's a windy windy day - with snow on the ground and cars making crunchy sounds as they go by. Little stray flakes of snow that forgot to come down last night are being spilled out now, and sort of dancing around, reluctant to settle down with the rest of them. It's a nice sort of day for talking, for sitting cozily by the fire - while the wind rattles the shutters and makes weird sounds around the corners of the house and moans in the trees. It's a nice day to stay by the fire, and when evening comes to pull a little table before the fireplace, and eat baked apples from amber plates - with just the firelight and a twinkly candle in a carved brass holder - to throw lights and shadows on the face of the one you love - to stay there through the evening talking, and perhaps reading a bit - out loud - a bit of favorite verse - or prose - and then dreaming - and feeling your hand clasped tight, as the embers die out...

This feeling I have for you . . . I can't conceive of it ending . . . before I couldn't see how anything couldn't end - at least after millions of years . . . now . . . do you understand?

Your Ede[2]

One of the nicest things about writing such loving letters, reflected Edith, was of course that Fran wrote her back...

[1] Schaeffer, *Tapestry*, 147.
[2] Schaeffer, *Tapestry*, 148.

Chapter 6

Fran's letters to Edith were just as loving but much less poetic.

Baby:

Greetings m'love, I love you. I wanted to be with you the last couple of days. We have had a holiday since Tuesday one o'clock and it is bad to have time with nothing to do. Wednesday we were supposed to have off, but then good old Dr. Bagby died and so we had two more days off. I am glad I had his full course last year. He was a great man but if he had had love in his life he would have been greater.

...Old dear, I love you. I did better than I expected, and got first honor roll again. Unlimited cuts! My average was 91 2/3, I heard it was the best in the junior class, but I'm not sure. Greek 86. Fair lady, I lay my laurels at your feet. They are yours.

So my folks gave you some of my "boy" pictures. I'm glad you like him. He is an odd fellow, but sometimes I think I like him better than the older boy he grew into. Still the older boy has one joy in his life that supersedes all the minor traits he has lost...- your love.

I hope we shall have such a boy, but one who will be very very much better because of your share in his personality. I would liked to have seen you blush when Dad called you Mrs. Schaeffer Jr. I will be glad to see you write it for the first time after we are married. I love you, dearest person. . . .

Franz[1]

And yet another letter came from Fran that same day!

Edith dearest:

Speaking of a letter every day, here are two in one day! Did you get my Special?...alas and alack, what goes up must come down, and I feel a siege of the "blues" coming on. With all your Home Ec do you know a long distance cure for such an illness? Possibly the cake, if it arrives tomorrow, will help,

---

[1] Schaeffer, *Tapestry*, 148-9.

but the kisses brought by the cake may make me want a few of the real thing - woe is me! I love you.

...I'm sorry the Special had to be rushed - I didn't get nearly all that I wanted to say in it...How did you like the change to "baby" on the special? You see how you have me wrapped around your finger? One word from you and I hasten to obey, do I not, old woman? Ha, ha. I love you.

Did I tell you I was elected vice-president of the lit society, and secretary of the Ministerial Association? If I did I'm not trying to make a little seem a lot by repeating -but if not I don't want to keep any secrets from my wife! Now goodnight and I wish I were kissing you. . . .

Franz[1]

Edith answered from her friend's apartment in Plainfield:

Dearest . . .

There are so many things I want to kiss you about!! First you're special. When the mail came at home this morning, and there was no familiar scrawl for me, my heart sank to my toes for I had wanted terribly to hear. All the way on the train to Plainfield, I thought of you . . .

The fields were dazzling in whiteness - and soft piles of snow snuggled in the branches. Well . . .when I arrived Ellen was there all beaming to meet me. We went shopping, then to a cute tea room paneled in dark wood, for lunch, after which we shopped for things for dinner tonight, and came home laden with bulky parcels. The apartment house is swanky!! - As we opened the door - the first thing we saw was your special on the floor! And my heart went hippity hop - right up 'til it was soaring in the sky. Oh I love you. Then I read it - retiring to the bathroom to do so. It is a lovely bathroom tiled in the most heavenly shade of pale green. The letter was exactly what I needed. Thanks, darling, for coming to the rescue. My weekend is complete now...[2]

Edith answered yet again when she returned home:

...More congratulations! You deserve a telegram, but the budget won't allow it so my congratulations this way and a

---

[1] Schaeffer, *Tapestry,* 149-50.
[2] Schaeffer, *Tapestry,* 150-51.

kiss later! Vice-president-secretary-very fine. But don't let them overwork you. There's another association you are going to be "president" of you know, and that company wants you un-worn-out! I left my pen in Plainfield, isn't that dumb? So I'm using mother's. Sunday night I came home just because I love to ride a train at night. I love to hear it shriek - and feel it rushing through the blackness. I gave other reasons, but that was the real one. School again today. . . Sociology and History of Education are going to require heaps of reading. I see myself spending hours in the library this spring. I'm still thinking in terms of spring even though it is bitterly cold. . .

...War, War, war. . . There's so much talk about it or maybe I've been listening to the wrong programs. The international air seems full of it. Then Austria-France-Germany are getting tangled up. The good old U. S. A. is even getting wise enough to enlarge their Navy and Air fleets - it all gives me the queerest cold chills inside.

I love you...[1]

In 1934 Fran wrote:

Dearest Edith:
...here is something I want you to do for me when we are married; if I am ever slightly mad, and want to join some secular organization...do your best to keep me out of whatever I want to join! Even if it apparently would widen my influence, still shout this to me: No matter how good the organization is, if it is not primarily Christian, do not give allegiance to it. In a long run its lines will cross your Christian lines and it will also take time and energy for a lesser cause when the Greatest Cause needs all you have got to put into it...

...I enjoyed your Sunday letter very much. It helped me muchly. Your drawings, and the smell of flowers brought me your overflowing love of life. Edith, you are magnificent. How I won your love I do not know, but of the fact I am glad. . . You said about your not being brave, my last letter shows just how steady I am! We are non-brave when separated, but I am not afraid of our courage when we stand together...

---
[1] Schaeffer, *Tapestry*, 151-52.

No matter what my mood, the letter that arrives each day is a constant source of strength and joy. Please do as much as you can on them. I need them . . . the things you do, events around You, and most of all the things and words that retell me how much you love me. I am quite dependent on you. I find more all the time that this is so. Do you like that? I hope so, for I'll be more and more dependent on you all the rest of my life...I need my other half to make this half work well! I love you.

Franz[1]

Later, after hearing Howard Taylor of the China Inland Mission speak, Fran wrote Edith forcefully emphasizing Christ was first in his life and he intended to win souls for Christ. He asked Edith if she felt the same way. The two had been committed to each other for nearly two years. Very shaken, she replied:

First of all - I want you to know that I am glad! To have you in God's will - to have you live the life He has planned for you whether it be with me or not - to have Him come first - to have your love for Him Supreme - to have your love fully consecrated - is what I would rather have for you than anything else in the universe even tho' it may leave me entirely out. It's because I love you so -because I truly love you - and don't only love you to fill my needs for companionship, etc. that I want the very best for you. There is nothing more glorious than the position you have taken - that of putting Christ first, really first. And -Franz - I feel that I have come to the same point. I thought I had before, but I never really considered laying you on the altar because I felt God had given you to me, that He really meant us to be together. And now - I see - Not that I feel we are not meant to work together, but that He must know our love for Him comes first. . . so that we put no "ifs" in our surrender. And - I believe I have done this today, if never before. I am willing to go wherever He wants me-even alone - All my life since I have been tiny I have wanted His will for my life - but in little things I have clung - not willing to give them up. But I have one by one given up things. Yet . . . as I've prayed for His will saying I would be willing to go anywhere - to the ends of the earth - I have also

---

[1] Schaeffer, *Tapestry*, 152-54.

asked that He would give me a helpmate. When I loved and was loved by one who had the same purpose in life, I thought it was a direct answer to this prayer, and I really never faced the question of giving you up.

When I got your letter this morning, I must confess I wept. Why? I wasn't sure . . . I knew I was glad for your decisions yet the thing bewildered me since I had been thanking Him for giving us this "most perfect" human love... I read my Bible, prayed, read your letter again - and prayed some more. Then on my knees I gave up all for Him . . . and told Him that if it were His will - I would work alone... If it is to be together - our lives will be much more fruitful for having come to this point - we will know that He does come first - and that what we tell others is not merely "words" but something we have known ourselves. We will know the true meaning of the word "first" as we could not otherwise have known.

...And now Franz, I cannot say that I feel any definite call to work alone - my heart and mind are open - but I still feel God has brought us together - that He has given us this good thing. God is a loving Father and His goodness is wonderful. I feel He can use us together to glorify His Kingdom. I feel a praise in my heart for Him -who gives His children the best. But if you ever feel definitely called to work alone, know - that I have left our love in His hands. God doesn't have two right ways for us if He did bring us together - if He does mean us to marry -then He has a work for us, that can only be done together.

I love you
Edith[1]

In late 1934 she wrote Fran about John and Betty Stam. They were two missionaries much younger than her own parents but with similar backgrounds. They also had gone to China separately for the China Inland Mission and married there. Also stationed not far from Shanghai, the Stams were not yet thirty years old with one baby daughter Helen. The Communists, who were trying to take over in China, brutally executed the Stams! A Chinese pastor managed to save the baby. The news was chilling, not only because of the tragedy but because Communists supposedly were a threat only in the remote areas of China. Chiang Kai-shek, the leader who

---

[1] Schaeffer, *Tapestry*, 155-6.

had finally subdued the will of all the warlords to unite China, was intent on crushing the Communists. But fate intervened to save the Communists. Japan became very aggressive, moving into Manchuria and threatening China from the northeast. This diversion saved the Communists and they continued to grow in number through threats, lies and cold-blooded murder.

Fran was inflamed by the tragedy. In his next letter he railed against Communism. He still wrote about missionary work, but at least he now assumed Edith would be with him. "You and I and our children may face what the Stams faced...," he penned, "are you with me even to that?"[1] But Edith was more practical on that matter. Fran had not even started seminary. He hadn't yet graduated college! But he would soon graduate, so Edith wrote about the merits of particular seminaries. Once it had seemed a certainty Fran would choose J. Gresham Machen's Westminster Seminary in Philadelphia. But he had found recent graduates of Westminster too belligerent - 'chips on their shoulders' - even though he agreed with them theologically. Now what was he going to do?

Edith offered her advice:

> How are you, old squeedunk?...Wish I had a million dollars - and I'd build a seminary - and get all good professors - and good students without any "chips" when they graduated. I'd have them fight when necessary and shut up and be sweet when it was necessary. I'd have it unmixed in the conflict - standing for the right but not talking about it! . . . being very positive - believing thoroughly - but presenting all sides fairly - unprejudiced, never finding fault. I'd have it all rosy doing good to church and community, but making everybody feel comfortable and not sticking pins in any one . . . yet accomplishing the work of seeing that people had the chance to find the true Word of God. . . .
>
> Franz, Franz maybe I'm a fighting person but isn't the desire to test the message of a man - by the only yardstick we have, a desire to save people? . . . don't judge a Seminary by comparing the conversation of fresh graduates with that of older Christians who have been softened and have grown through years of Christian work. Probably those fellows aren't all fight either, but they're young. . . The Lord may be leading you to look into Bible Schools thru this dissatisfaction

---

[1] Schaeffer, *Tapestry*, 159.

with Westminster. I feel I'll always be in sympathy with Westminster, tho' don't worry I won't harp on it. I know you want the Lord's will and so do I. If His will for you lies in some other place of preparation, you will have my whole-hearted support of your decision (thru His guidance). I adore you sweetheart - I'll be praying much about this thing - pray for me too Franz...that the hot insistent feeling inside me may go, and that I may look at things more as you do...Pray please that I may never spoil things for us by being too dogged in stubbornness. I am afraid I can be nasty, like "cherry cider," you know - and I don't want to be...

Why can't I trust more for the future? Oh Franz . . . Franz I love you . . . goodnight dearest,

Edith[1]

Because of her parents activity with the China Inland Mission Edith was always well aware of the international scene. While America wrestled with the Great Depression in the 1930's the rest of the world seemed to be careening toward destruction. Totalitarian forces like Communism and Fascism seemed to grow everywhere. To add to the gloom George Seville was involuntarily retired in early 1935 by the mission society. Not only was it a blow to his ego but it brought a significant reduction in pay. That meant among other things that Edith would not be able to continue college. She lacked just one year. Her friends at school couldn't believe it. She was president of the Honor Council and yet she would not be returning? It seemed providential though because Fran graduated college in June. The two might have waited a year until Edith graduated college to get married. Now they did not have to wait.

'Would you love me without a B. A.?' she teased in a letter.[2]

Meanwhile Fran applied for a scholarship to Westminster Seminary. He ranked second in his college class academically, had glowing letters of recommendation from his professors and had a long list of student activities. He had been on the Student Christian Association cabinet, serving as treasurer his third year and its president his senior year. In successive years in the Union Philanthropic Literary Society he was secretary, vice president and president. He had also served in the Ministerial Association and the student Finance Board. He had competed for the track team all four

---

[1] Schaeffer, *Tapestry*, 160-1.

[2] Schaeffer, *Tapestry*, 164.

years. He also belonged to an honor society. Fran prayed that he would get a scholarship.

'Best of all I can get a housing allowance if I'm married,' he realized with joy.

But he lamented his shortcomings too. He prayed for strength and wisdom as well as always returning to the Bible - his standard for everything. He was sure he did not have the sweetness of a man "who really keeps Christ's two great commandments". He still fought pride and passion. He memorized Paul's great "love chapter," the 13th chapter of I Corinthians. Every time Fran got upset over things, fished for compliments or felt his pride threatened, he went over that chapter in his mind. It helped. Fran also believed he lacked resolve and courage to stand for the truth. He must fearlessly oppose the modernists in the church who constantly watered down the truth.

But the news that Fran received his scholarship to Westminster was dampened by ever greater turmoil in the Presbyterian church...

Chapter 7

"Good grief!" exclaimed Fran. "My church is going to defrock J. Gresham Machen, the head of my seminary!"

J. Gresham Machen and his colleagues had not only founded the Westminster Theological Seminary but in 1933 they founded the 'Independent Board for Presbyterian Foreign Missions'. Whereas the main body of the Presbyterian Church USA seemed willing to tolerate Machen's new conservative seminary they were furious that Machen intended to send his own missionaries throughout the world to carry the Presbyterian name. In a shocking development the New Brunswick Presbytery found Machen guilty of violation of his ordination vow, of disapproval of the government and discipline in the Presbyterian Church USA, of renouncing and disobeying the rules and lawful authority of the Church, of advocating rebellious defiance against this authority, of refusing to sever his ties with the Independent Board, and of not being zealous and faithful in maintaining the peace of the Church.

"What does this mean to the seminary?" gasped Fran in disbelief.

In response Machen and his colleagues at Westminster scurried to form a new church. Machen had wanted to strengthen his church with conservative Bible-believing pastors from his Westminster Seminary. He had never wanted to leave his church. Now it seemed certain the guilty verdict would be upheld in 1936 by the General Assembly of the Presbyterian Church USA. Machen's new church would be called Presbyterian Church of America. It would become official just about the same day Fran was going to graduate from Hampden-Sydney! What was Fran getting into? He mulled over the correctness of what Machen and the others at Westminster were doing. Should church officials stay within the church and fight a rearguard action? Or should they bolt the church and start a new church? History had great men and women doing both. Some stayed. Some bolted. Fran decided to remain in the Presbyterian Church USA until its General Assembly made a final determination on the fate of Machen.

"But I will attend Machen's seminary," he realized. "And best of all I'm going to marry Edith this summer!"

The Sevilles encouraged the marriage. The same was not true for the Schaeffers. Fran's father - whom Edith already called 'Pop' - was not opposed but mother Bessie was. Bessie had not married until Frank could afford to get married. So how could Fran get married if he was still a student? Bessie was so upset she said she would not attend the wedding. Edith visited the Schaeffers often and Bessie seemed to constantly sting her with nasty remarks. Edith tried hard to forgive Bessie and put it behind her, but the abuse hurt.

Finally Edith went with the Schaeffers to Hampden-Sydney in early June. Fran was to graduate in a ritual ending only after four days! But the college had refined the ritual to perfection. The atmosphere remained charged on the campus lush with flowers. It climaxed in the church as the graduates filed in.

Frank Schaeffer grunted a whisper. "What's all that pile of white rolls tied up in ribbon?"

Edith whispered back, "They're the diplomas, Pop. They prove they have their degrees."

Frank found Fran's name on the program. "He's got three of those names beside his. That's better than two, isn't it?"

"Yes, Pop, Fran's getting his Bachelor of Arts magna cum laude, and that is great. He has done so well."

Frank had another surprise. When Fran received his diploma the college president announced Fran had been selected for the 'Algernon Sydney Sullivan Award' as the 'outstanding Christian on the campus during his four years'.[1] For that he received a medallion and a plaque. After the ceremony he received a kiss from a very proud Edith. Both knew that shortly they would experience an even greater event in their lives: marriage.

Reality hit Edith back in Germantown when she stopped at her friend Dot's house to pick up a book. Edith's best friends at Beaver College surprised her with a shower. She sat on the living room floor opening package after package of mainly items for the kitchen. Meanwhile Fran began working for a bakery. Part of his pay would be a cake for the wedding! Edith made a white lace peplum blouse to add to a white crepe evening gown she had already made as a class project. That would be her wedding dress. Her mother helped her make bridesmaids' dresses for her sisters Janet and Elsa.

Meanwhile Fran was collecting furniture for their apartment too. Some he salvaged. They had found a third-floor apartment on

---

[1] Schaeffer, *Tapestry,* 141.

Greene Street in Philadelphia. The Art Museum was nearby but the neighborhood was rundown. The shabby apartment had four rooms, all diminutive: living-dining room, bedroom, bathroom, and kitchen. It also opened onto a tin roof. But at least that offered Edith an easy way to occasionally get out in the sun, if she didn't mind looking down into some seedy backyards. Westminster Seminary was then located on Pine Street, just a good walk from their apartment. But none of that would happen until September.

"Because after the wedding we will be camp counselors at Camp Michidune in Michigan," Edith told her astonished friends.

Edith's father married them in the Wayne Avenue United Presbyterian Church on July 6, 1935. Because her father didn't want to walk down the aisle with her, then change places, he had his friend Paul Wooley, Professor of Church History of Westminster Seminary, give Edith away. Best man was Richard Gaffin, also from Westminster. Gaffin and his wife had decorated the church with wild flowers. Edith was a whirlwind of activity. As guests were arriving - including Bessie Schaeffer - Edith was still making floral wreaths for herself and her sisters to wear in their hair! She even made the bridesmaids' bouquets. Her own bridal bouquet was donated by a Christian florist. The ceremony itself proved a somber, nervous one because Fran and Edith took their vows to God very seriously. But after the ceremony the tension evaporated. Music, flowers, food and friends made it a very festive occasion.

"Good luck," screamed celebrants later as Fran and Edith clattered off in his Model A.

They had little money. They could buy gas and rent motel rooms but that was all. So they took food, dishes and a hot plate. On the way to their first motel stop they impulsively stopped to have chocolate milk shakes. Edith stained her beautiful white traveling suit that she had labored on for a long time. She had to try very hard not to let that spoil the moment. And what a moment it was. It was her first real separation from her parents. The newlyweds traveled north, stopping each night at a motel along the way until they reached Cleveland. There they stayed with Edith's Aunt Bess. They ate royally: fried chicken, salad, fresh peas, and hot biscuits with several varieties of Aunt Bess's home-made jams and jellies.

After two weeks they arrived at Camp Michidune. They made little money above subsistence but the experience with raucous children was valuable. Edith had been apprehensive about teaching leather craft but that seemed trivial after she learned she had to teach lifesaving! She must have taught herself well because once while life-guarding she actually towed a floundering girl to safety! That summer to save money she also began to cut Fran's hair. He was so pleased he insisted she cut his hair from then on.

The Schaeffers were allowed to stay together in the attic room of a Summer Bible Conference building a short walk from the camp. This was a far cry from Edith's 'garret in Paris' she had daydreamed about as a teenager. They had two very narrow, canvas cots with the thinnest of mattresses. There was nothing else in the room but two straight-back chairs and a tiny cupboard rattling with a handful of wire hangers. The room was uninhabitable during the daytime because of the heat. Nevertheless Edith made a pair of decorative stools to sit on. The tiny room was their first 'home'.

"The 'slum apartment' that awaits us in Philadelphia in September now seems like a mansion!" said Edith brightly.

Edith may have mastered new skills of leather craft, life saving and barbering that summer but she did not master driving a car. On the way back to Pennsylvania she became distracted gawking at sights and rammed the Model A into the rear of another car. Edith was lucky that she had been driving slow and that in those days cars had large protruding bumpers. If cars collided at low speed usually one bumper overrode the other and they 'locked'. Then someone, just as Fran did that day, had to bounce up and down on the bumpers until they parted. There was no permanent damage to either car. Fran apologized profusely to the other driver. But he was furious with Edith for her careless driving.

"I'll never drive again," grumped Edith.

If Fran was so volatile over his car she would just let him drive. In fact, they had discovered they both had hot tempers. Edith reacted more often than Fran but usually with sarcasm. Fran reacted less often but more intensely, and with less self control. Edith decided it really was best to remove sources of friction whenever possible. She told herself Fran could not only drive back to Philadelphia but drive forever after!

Their tempers were calmed by the time they reached Philadelphia. The seedy apartment looked wonderful after a summer in a tiny attic room. For their bedroom Fran refinished the dresser, chest of drawers and iron bedstead with cream-colored paint. Edith added leather handles to the drawers, curtains and a new bedspread to match. Every night Fran studied by setting up a card table in the bedroom. Edith was in the living room laboring on her White sewing machine or working leather.

She said later, "I did dressmaking, and I designed, made and sold leather belts and buttons. The proceeds went to purchase our food and gas and so on - just enough to squeak through."[1]

The young couple kept the apartment spotless. Every week the two polished the furniture, washed the windows, scrubbed and waxed floors, and shook out the small rag rugs on the roof. Fran also helped with the washing. Here the tin roof was a boon because it had clothes lines.

Fran lugged two tubs to the roof, which he filled with dirt. "Next spring we will add a roof garden to our penthouse!" he promised.

Part of their daily ritual during the week was for Fran to make breakfast, then pack two identical lunches. The lunches consisted of a different kind of sandwich for each day of the week plus a packet of celery sticks, carrot sticks, raisins or some other fruit or vegetable. Fran wanted them to eat the same thing in the same amount so they would have the same feelings when it came time for dinner! And of course Edith wanted them to eat their lunches - Fran in the seminary on Pine Street and Edith in the apartment at Greene Street - at exactly the same time. Her reasoning for this she had advanced years before when they both read *Daily Light* - Fran in Virginia and Edith in Pennsylvania - at exactly the same of the day.

"We are bonded in time, even when apart."

Edith also insisted on staying up just as late as Fran did. If he studied until three o'clock in the morning she worked at hand sewing or leather craft until three in the morning. She did no machine sewing while Fran studied because the noise could be distracting. Often Fran would run ideas past Edith. After all, she was very well versed in Christian doctrine. Edith enjoyed that immensely. But she did not enjoy Hebrew. Fran had to memorize a huge vocabulary off cards. That meant total silence. For Edith. Meanwhile Fran muttered Hebrew to himself!

His Hebrew professor was Allan MacRae, who quite naturally also taught Old Testament. The rest of the faculty included Machen, Cornelius Van Til, Stonehouse, Oswald Allis, Kuiper, Wooley, and John Murray. Van Til influenced Fran most. He was 50, a Dutch immigrant to America at the age 10, and fiery. He taught apologetics, the defense of Christianity. He had been greatly influenced by

---

[1] Schaeffer, *Tapestry*, 185.

reading Dutch theologians as well as studying under B. B. Warfield at Princeton. Apologetics was a complex discipline. First, one had to decide which system of discerning truth was best. Many theologians did not articulate this at all. But its articulation was very important in the Westminster sphere.

"Van Til makes sure of that," Fran told Edith.

Three systems were recognized: evidentialism, verificationism and presuppositionalism. Evidentialism, also called induction or empiricism, was a classic approach of observing particulars in order to generalize, even to approximate, truths. Presuppositionalism, or deduction, was a method that first assumed certain premises were true, then tested all facts for truth in that context. Verificationism, or the so-called scientific method, worked from a hypothesis to test facts for the truth. Although verificationism seemed very similar to presuppositionalism, it was actually much looser, employing both inductive and deductive methods.

Fran tended, as many did, to be a verificationist. But Cornelius Van Til was a presuppositionalist. He insisted one had to think from two premises: 1. The Creator of everything was the Trinity. 2. Nonbelievers will resist the premise. Although it seemed Van Til had set as truth what he was trying to prove, by sheer energy and ferocity he usually convinced his listeners he was right - until they escaped his domination. In any event, the field of apologetics was argumentative by definition but thought-provoking. And it gave the seminary student some tools to later battle the 'world'.

Also in seminary Fran really learned what his church was all about. "Necessary information since we seem to fight constantly over particulars."

Just how was his church different from other Protestant denominations? Like many other churches it had a very solemn worship. Like many others it had only two sacraments: baptism and communion. It was certainly similar in its beliefs to many other denominations but its distinguishing feature was its organization, of which the most distinctive body, the presbytery, was the source for the church's name. The local group was a 'session', led by an ordained pastor and a group of 'ruling elders', all of whom had been elected by the lay people of the congregation. Some of the congregation were 'deacons', who usually performed day-to-day tasks of the church. The session had the power to 'to admonish, to rebuke, to suspend or exclude from the sacraments,' and, in general 'to concert the best measures for promoting the spiritual interests of the congregation'.[1]

The next level of government, the presbytery - that so distinguished Fran's denomination - 'consists of all the ministers, in number no less than five, and one ruling elder from each congregation, within a certain district.' The presbytery has the power 'to receive and issue all appeals, complaints and references that are regularly brought before it from church sessions...to examine and license candidates for the holy ministry; to ordain, install, remove, and judge ministers; to examine and approve or censure the records of church sessions; to resolve questions of doctrine or discipline seriously and reasonably proposed; to condemn erroneous opinions which injure the purity or peace of the Church; to visit particular churches, for the purpose of inquiring into their state and redressing the evils that may have arisen in them; to unite or divide congregations, at the request of the people, or to form or receive new congregations, and, in general, to order whatever pertains to the spiritual welfare of the churches under their care.'[2]

"So the real power in our denomination is in its presbyteries," mulled Fran, "not in the higher levels of synod and General Assembly."

Fran and Edith often met with the professors and their wives. In addition the Schaeffers knew Westminster's registrar Laird Harris, who was also a budding authority on the Bible, and his wife Libby. Other friends included fellow student Doug Young and his wife Snook. The Youngs' apartment was not only in the same building but just one floor below. Edith could go down the fire escape and knock on Snook's kitchen door! Snook had interests similar to Edith's, not only Westminster but dressmaking, cooking and the international situation. All seminary students and their wives knew missionary work was a possibility. Fran and Edith often gazed at a world map. On their kitchen wall was a map of China, autographed by Howard Taylor of the China Inland Mission. On the map Fran added 'Serve the Lord with gladness'.[3]

Fran and Edith learned other student families were also troubled by the contention within their own church. It seemed unfair that

---

[1] John A. Hardon, *The Protestant Churches of America*. (NY: Image Books, 1969), 197.

[2] Hardon, *Protestant Churches of America*, 197.

[3] Schaeffer, *Tapestry*, 187.

standing for holiness and Biblical truths seemed to lead to strife and unpleasantness. Another troubling thing was one tenet of their Reformed faith. As Calvinists they believed everything had been predetermined by God. The troubling aspect of that was just how much free will did they then have? None? Some? Or, somehow, complete free will? The question was by no means academic. It was only too prominent in the religious life at Westminster. Edith was scolded by a professor's wife for praying for something specific. 'God works out the details' was her implication. It was not right to bother Him with specifics. This view was one Edith had rarely encountered, even though she had been raised in a pastor's family. Yes, the Westminster crowd was zealous for their Calvinist faith.

Yet American Presbyterians had actually compromised on the ticklish subject of predestination and its bearing on salvation in 1903. The Westminster Confession of Faith, drafted by English Puritans in 1646, read "By the decree of God, for the manifestation of his glory, some men and angels are predestined unto everlasting life, and others foreordained to everlasting death." So that no one would see a loophole in that statement the 1646 Confession added that no others are "redeemed by Christ, effectually called, justified, adopted, sanctified, and saved but the elect only. The rest of mankind, God was pleased, according to the unsearchable counsel of his own will . . . to ordain them to dishonor and wrath for their sin, to the praise of his glorious justice."[1]

In 1903 the Presbyterian Church U.S.A. widened the gate to salvation by adding, "Concerning those who perish, the doctrine of God's eternal decree is held in harmony with the doctrine that God desires not the death of any sinner, but has provided in Christ a salvation sufficient for all...men are fully responsible for their treatment of God's gracious offer...his decree hinders no man from accepting that offer...no man is condemned except on the ground of his sin." They further added, "All who put their trust in Christ face divine judgment without fear..."[2] The 1903 modification seemed to contradict the 1646 doctrine. Yet the church could not get the necessary votes to expunge the 1646 doctrine. So the contradiction remained. Perhaps it was just as well to prevent further splintering of the church over yet some other issue. For the Presbyterians were fighting over many issues.

---

[1] Hardon, *Protestant Churches of America*, 192-3.
[2] Hardon, *Protestant Churches of America*, 193.

After church on Sundays Fran and Edith usually visited Germantown - one set of parents for lunch and afternoon, followed by the other set of parents for supper and evening. The next week they would reverse the order. Invariably the parents would insist they take food back to their apartment. Of course the young couple needed outings alone too. Often Fran and Edith took long walks in Fairmont Park. But most of their life revolved around the seminary with all its joys and strife. Fran's very high marks in his first year of classes reassured them it was worthwhile.

In the summer of 1936 the two once again went to camp but this time they were in charge. Camp Richard Webber Oliver - sponsored by the evangelical New England Fellowship - was in Rumney, New Hampshire. The White Mountains offered both scenery and the pleasures of hiking and climbing. Fran and Edith, strangers to mountains, were enthralled. They ran a camp for young boys. But the fun and games were soured for Fran and Edith by the news that J. Gresham Machen had indeed been defrocked by the General Assembly of Presbyterian Church USA. Carl MacIntire, one of his proteges, had also been defrocked.

"I must resign from the Presbyterian Church USA," sighed Fran.

Fran wrote a letter of resignation immediately. Back at Westminster that fall - as a member of Machen's Presbyterian Church of America - Fran resumed his studies. But that fall of 1936 brought yet another major developments to the young couple...

Chapter 8

"I'm going to have a baby," Edith told Fran.

Edith worked harder than ever at sewing to build a nest egg for the baby's arrival. If customers furnished the material she made them well-tailored clothing, like a fully lined winter coat for $8 or a long dress with rolled-hem ruffles for $5. Then their financial situation worsened. That fall Fran had to have an emergency operation for appendicitis. Suddenly they had the financial burden of medical expenses for the operation and the required two-week hospital stay. In addition the immobility severely hampered Fran's studies. Edith had to spend the entire evening copying John Young's seminary class notes, then take them to Fran the next morning - in spite of morning sickness.

"Thanks," said Fran sheepishly from his hospital bed.

Was it any wonder he could not imagine life without Edith? Even when Fran was released he was not allowed to go back to seminary for one month. One day in January 1937 Fran was in the apartment taking a test sent to him by Professor Machen when he got shocking news. Machen was dead! How could that be? He was only 56. He had gone on a speaking tour of churches in the northern tier of states to promote the Presbyterian Church of America. He fought a bad cold, yet kept engagements anyway. His cold slipped into pneumonia. In North Dakota he had to be hospitalized.

His last words were reported to be 'I am so thankful for the active obedience of Christ.'

Machen - the giant - had held the contentious elements of the Westminster Seminary together. He was also the glue for the new Presbyterian Church of America. What would happen now? Fran and Edith had little time to reflect. Their own problems were pressing. The bills for Fran's illness - totaling what seemed an astronomical 75 dollars - would deplete Edith's nest egg for the baby. After much fervent prayer to God for a very specific 75 dollars Edith went to the hospital office that handled payments. She explained their precarious financial situation to the administrator. He explained they had a fund for just such needs. In fact they had exactly 75 dollars! She left, owing the hospital nothing!

Remembering the scolding from the professor's wife, Edith had to say, "Never have I had such proof that God does indeed answer our very specific prayers!"

Fran was back in good health as birth of the baby approached in June. But nothing was ever normal in their lives now. Contention - that might have been subdued under Machen - raged at the seminary. Much of the dispute originated from a power struggle but outwardly crystallized in two major issues. One was the issue for personal liberties or 'Christian liberties'. In late 1933 prohibition of alcohol had been repealed. Americans could drink alcohol again legally. But many in the church insisted it was intolerable, along with tobacco, dancing, card playing and other 'frivolous' un-Biblical behavior. There was much disagreement within the seminary on the issue, though the majority did not see alcohol and dancing as sinful within themselves. Fran sided with the minority, getting very worked up over the issue, just like all the others. Soon Edith, fueled by Fran's anger, was also riled.

The second issue was the 'End Time'. The 19th century had been a time of progress, a time that generated optimism. But the 20th century with its bloody World War I, followed a decade later by worldwide economic depression, was not a time of optimism. The world seemed in decline, and the rise of aggressive Fascism in Germany, Italy and Japan and of Godless Communism in Russia only reinforced that impression. This pessimism rejuvenated a view of End Times called 'dispensational premillenialism'. This view saw the world getting worse and worse until the Second Coming of Christ. In the 19th century most church people regarded that view as a refuge for crackpots. But the horrible events of the 20th century changed all that. More and more church people accepted it. Naturally the zealots at Westminster argued about it.

'Although the Bible is true it is not exhaustive,' many admitted, including Fran.

So the two divisive issues could be argued either way. But that did not mean feelings could be salved or the issues shelved because the issues had to resolved in order to spell out the new church's doctrine. They needed a peacemaker and there was none. Van Til was no 'elder statesman' but an elder firebrand. After a heated meeting in May 1937 on the two issues several professors in the minority on 'Christian liberty' and premillenialism decided to bolt!

"Yet another new church and moreover a new seminary!" observed Fran in a daze.

Samuel Laird had made the new splinter group possible. He offered the rebellious professors the use of his First Independent Church facilities in Wilmington, Delaware, just across the river from Philadelphia. It seemed a bizarre dream. When the fall 1937 term began there would be a 'Bible Presbyterian Church' and a 'Faith Theological Seminary'. The caliber of the new seminary faculty headed by Allan MacRae gave it instant credibility. For the revolt also included Carl MacIntire, Laird Harris, Roy Brumbaugh and Fred Paist. Among the 25 bolting students were Doug Young and Francis Schaeffer. In fact, Fran was the first student to register at Faith Theological Seminary. Because the rebels were in the minority many uninformed assumed that Westminster seminary and the Presbyterian Church of America remained staunchly Reformed and Calvinist - the seminary and the church that Machen founded. The uninformed saw the rebel Faith seminary Bible Presbyterian church as fundamentalist!

However Fran, like the other rebels, thought differently. "We represent the true Calvinist, Reformed Church."

Because of Edith's condition there would be no camp counseling jobs for the Schaeffers in the summer of 1937. Allan MacRae, who was to be president of the new seminary, hired Fran for the summer. The two had much to do for the opening term. Once in early June Edith experienced 'labor pains' and Fran rushed her to the hospital in his Model A. He was stopped by a policeman for speeding but the sight of Edith changed the arrest into a police-escort race to the hospital. But after a night of anxiety the doctor pronounced the episode 'false labor'.

Fran, still occasionally unable to control his temper, indulged his anger. He couldn't understand why Edith did not know the pains were false. After that Edith was determined to wait for the right moment. On June 18 she and Fran were having supper with the Sevilles. Her water burst. Again she was rushed to the hospital. This time of course it was the real thing. But it was an ordeal. Edith knew nothing about breathing techniques to help child birth. She tensed up and fought the painful process. After several hours of labor she was rushed into the delivery room. An ether mask was slapped over her face to put her to sleep and she fought that too. Fran, in the waiting room, was startled to see a nurse rush out of the delivery room weeping.

"What happened?" he stammered.

He only learned later that baby Priscilla was born at 11:20 PM but was not breathing! In the delivery room the doctor tried one method after another to revive the baby girl. Finally he gave mouth-to-mouth resuscitation. It worked! Once again a persistent, highly skilled doctor had come to Edith's rescue. Mothers remained in the hospital two weeks in those days. So Edith and the baby Priscilla recuperated in bed while Fran toiled with Allan MacRae at the seminary.

Just one month later Edith insisted on helping launch the new seminary. Fran's job was to find lodging for the students and faculty. So with Priscilla safely with the Sevilles Edith rode in the Model A with Fran around Wilmington. It was a major task because Fran was supposed to buy the housing! They were lucky enough to find lodging just two blocks from the church. Fran made down payments on *four* very large three-story frame houses. But the four houses would require considerable remodeling to make separate rooms and apartments. However, this was no barrier for Fran.

"Thanks to Pop's tutelage I can tackle just about any remodeling, plumbing, wiring or carpentry problem," he said immodestly.

He knew how to scrounge. He had little money to work with, so he found what he needed at junk yards: sinks, stoves, toilet bowls, wash basins. He could only do so much himself, so he hired people to help with plumbing and wiring. He knew how to supervise too. Next he purchased used furniture. Edith's contribution at his point was to find affordable bolts of cloth to make curtains and slipcovers. With Edith's help Fran did the impossible. Lodging would be ready for the occupants in September.

The Schaeffers moved in earlier. It was a rainy August day when a truck took most of their furniture from Greene Street. Then Fran, Edith and two-month-old Priscilla left in the Model A, loaded to the ceiling. It had already been a very long, trying day. During the drive to Wilmington the baby had an explosive bout of diarrhea. The diaper was no barrier at all. The stench in the closed car was more than Fran could bear. He lost his temper.

"Don't you even know how to put on diapers?" he raged at Edith.[1]

Suddenly the red-faced Fran stomped on the brakes but the Model A skidded on the wet pavement and hit the rear end of another car. Edith waited for volcanic Fran to really erupt. But he

---

[1] Schaeffer, *Tapestry*, 198.

didn't. He calmly got out to inspect the damage. As was so often the case in those days of huge bumpers there was no damage. Fran helped unlock the bumpers, calmly got in and drove on to Wilmington. Edith waited for him to talk, mystified by his sudden serenity.

"Right when that collision happened," he finally said, "Hebrews 12: 11 flashed into my mind."

Edith knew Hebrews 12:11. 'No discipline seems pleasant at the time, but painful. Later on, however, it produces a harvest of righteousness and peace for those who have been trained by it.'

Fran continued, "I believe with all my heart and soul God brought me up short with that collision - chastened me - for losing my temper and striking out unfairly yet once again."

And Edith noticed after that incident in the car that Fran did try much harder to control his temper. He also knew Ephesians 4:26: "In your anger do not sin." But in the past the intense zeal he had for everything often exploded into anger. Now he still fumed and seethed often. Even occasionally he could not control his rage. But afterward, he was always very remorseful, asking for forgiveness. At least his remorse was a great gift for Edith. Another great gift she received that year was the nearness of her parents. George Seville had been hired to teach Greek at the seminary. The Sevilles actually lived in the very housing that Fran and Edith had just refurbished. In addition, Jessie Seville often led the wives' prayer meeting.

While most of the women had toiled as faculty wives Jessie had been more like the great missionary C. T. Studd, who declared, 'Some wish to live within the sound of church and chapel bell. I wish to run a rescue mission within a yard of hell!'[1]

The church building where they held the Faith Theological Seminary classes was just across the street from the Baltimore and Ohio Railroad Station. As serious as the students were they could not restrain themselves when the magnificent Royal Blue Express - nonstop from New York to Washington, D.C. - went blazing past. They rushed to the windows to watch the streamliner. In many ways 1937 was still an age of innocence.

In May 1938 Fran graduated from Faith Theological Seminary, having made straight As. He had the honor to be the *first* ordained pastor of the Bible Presbyterian Church. But best of all he would at long last be a pastor! 'First in dignity' was the pastor, traditionally

---

[1] Edyth Draper etal, editors, *Almanac of the Christian World*.
(Wheaton, Illinois: Tyndale House Publishers, 1992), 731.

given many titles by his church. He was bishop, pastor, minister, elder, ambassador, angel of the Church, and steward of the mysteries of God. What a responsibility!

During the ceremony Edith was especially thrilled to hear the seminary students singing "Give Tongues of Fire to Preach Thy Word". 'What a plea to the Lord!' she thought, tears streaming down her cheeks. 'What a longing in hearts of young men!'[1]

The Schaeffers who left seminary in 1938 were quite a different family than the newlyweds who had started seminary in September 1935. Fran was a pastor, and a much mellowed one at that. Edith was a pastor's wife and a mother. Priscilla, only a dream in 1935, was now a toddler of almost one year. The Schaeffers had not realized their dream of evangelizing in China or some other exotic place. No, they moved to Grove City, Pennsylvania, 350 miles west of Philadelphia. It was a small town north of Pittsburgh.

'In a way though I've come home,' thought Edith.

She had noticed how often new paths cross old paths in a tapestry, woven by the Great Designer. In 1844 her great-grandfather Jacob Crooks and great-grandmother Nancy McRoberts Crooks of Saintfield, County Downs, North Ireland, settled on a farm near the Allegheny River north of Pittsburgh. They had two children at the time, one of whom, 3-year-old Eliza Jane, was to be George Seville's mother. Nancy Crooks was a legend in the family, her retorts so quick and tart they had been recorded.

When Jacob complained because she ran out of flour she snapped, 'Aren't you glad you lived to see the last of it!'

Of a compulsive housekeeper she quipped, 'She made up all the beds in the house before anybody was up.'[2]

In that same area the Sevilles were already there. John Seville, born in Manchester, England, had come to Pittsburgh in 1819 when he was 30. The Civil War hammered the Sevilles, with John and three of his sons dying. But one son, also named John, survived the Civil War. John Seville married Eliza Jane Crooks. One of their offspring was Edith's father, George. So Edith felt very much as if she had lived there in western Pennsylvania before.

Two elders of the church in Grove City came to Wilmington in a truck to help Pastor Francis Schaeffer move. The Schaeffers followed the truck in their Model A. The Covenant Presbyterian

---

[1] Schaeffer, *Tapestry*, 200.
[2] Schaeffer, *Tapestry*, 68.

Church in Grove City consisted of 18 rebels who had left the regular Presbyterian Church because it was too liberal. They met in the American Legion Hall. The Schaeffers would live next door in a building with eight apartments. Their first-floor apartment had a kitchen and three rooms. Fran's salary was exactly $100 a month. After rent and insurance Edith had $45 at her disposal every month. Precocious Priscilla immediately made an impression. She dumped all their medical supplies into the toilet and flushed them.

Edith had to tell Fran, "Not only are our supplies lost but the toilet overflowed..."

Sunday morning was a nervous time - Fran's first sermon. The church was in an upstairs meeting hall in the American Legion. The 18 members included no children. The children had been left - at their own insistence - with their friends in the Sunday School of the regular Presbyterian Church. Edith prayed Priscilla would be good, or at least quiet. Edith did not pray for Fran, but prayed instead that the Holy Spirit would speak through him. This became her practice. She never allowed a spat to contaminate her thoughts. It was essential that Fran convey the truth to the congregation through the Holy Spirit. She never believed that a pastor was limited by his own frailties. Could he preach about a problem he had himself? Yes.

"Because hopefully it is the Holy Spirit talking, not him," she believed.

The sermon went well, but a church without any child but his own one-year-old Priscilla was unacceptable to Fran. He wasn't about to be heavy-handed and harangue the congregation to bring their children. He would win the children. It was summer and what better time for a wienie roast? He found a fine clearing in the town's forested city park. He bought hot dogs, buns, marshmallows and pop. Then he did something astonishing. He got in his Model A and began rounding up boys!

"Hey, you kids want to go to a wienie roast?" he would call out to some boys playing marbles.

"How about some hot dogs and pop?" he would call to some boys playing baseball in an empty lot.

Soon he delivered 17 boys to the park!

By the time the roast was over Fran had fed the boys and delivered a nice easy talk about creation. The boys voiced their approval by calling Fran 'Rev'. Yes, they shouted, they did want a next time! And so the roast went on week after week, usually drawing about 20 boys. These boys became the nucleus of Fran's two-week Summer Bible School. With their help Fran went door-to-door talking to parents and inviting children to his Bible School. The result was phenomenal.

"Seventy-nine!" gasped Edith the first morning of Bible School.

They ranged in age from five years to the teen years. It was a good thing Edith's mother had come to help. The children included girls now. And the number swelled to 100 before the two weeks of school was over. Still, Edith was not astonished that Fran had captivated the children of the small town in such a short time. She had seen him in action at the summer camps they had counseled. He had become masterful with children. He knew how to let kids have fun. And in their fun he reached them with his message. Their closing program for Bible School was a huge success. They put on a show for parents and relatives. There was nothing solemn about it either. It too was great fun. Edith was thrilled that several children had come to Christ during the two weeks.

"Mother and I helped but it was Fran's innovative and winning ways that had made it possible."

But in spite of the great success few of the children came to Sunday School and fewer yet came to church. Still, Fran and Edith persisted. They held similar parties for students at Grove City College and inspired a few to attend church or youth meetings they hosted in their apartment. They opened a chapter of 'The Miracle Book Club', a home Bible study program for high schoolers. Although the Schaeffers remained relatively poor they rented a beat-up old house. They were never afraid of 'fixer-uppers'. The size of the house would allow larger in-home get-togethers.

"When we aren't hosting meetings in the evenings we can refinish furniture," agreed the energetic twosome.

Fran even took furniture with him when he called on people. As he talked he sanded! Growth of the congregation was slow but steady. Within two years it had reached 100. When Fran found out that a small white clapboard church stood abandoned in a valley that was going to be flooded he convinced the 'session' to buy it. It even had four stain-glassed windows. They took the old church apart piece by piece and rebuilt it on a lot in Grove City. But only Fran and one other fearless man would climb up the towering ladder to paint the steeple!

One day in 1940 Fran heard his mother on the phone. "Pop's had a stroke, come quick."[1]

Fran rushed to Germantown and the old home on Ross Street. His father was in bed. But his mind was sharp. He asked Fran at long last to bring him to Jesus. For the first time ever his father listened with real eagerness. Fran explained without church jargon just what belief in Christ meant. By the time Fran left his old home Pop was born again. When the older Schaeffers visited Grove City later that year Fran and Edith insisted they sleep in their bedroom. But any inconvenience was quickly forgotten. Because the older Schaeffers insisted on giving them brand new electric appliances.

"A washing machine and a refrigerator!" cried Edith.

By the time the new church building was dedicated, the congregation numbered 110. Fran had preached in Grove City for three years. Then in that same year of 1941 Fran was asked to come to Chester, Pennsylvania, and preach as a "candidate" for their assistant pastorship. The Chester congregation was very large. Moreover, Chester was a town on the southern fringe of Philadelphia. Fran and Edith would be near their aging parents and their old friends and colleagues at Faith Seminary.

Fran and Edith decided he must become a candidate. ...

---

[1] Schaeffer, *Tapestry*, 210.

Chapter 9

As the Schaeffers awaited word from Chester, their daughter Susan was born at 6:20 A.M. on May 28, 1941. Then Fran was offered the assistant pastorship in Chester. He accepted. The Grove City newspaper reported his departure with the headline COVENANT PASTOR TO PREACH LAST SERMON SUNDAY:

> Rev. F. A. Schaeffer, Covenant Presbyterian Church pastor, has been called to associate pastor of the Bible Presbyterian Church of Chester, Pa., unaffiliated, and has accepted the call...Rev. Schaeffer is moderator of the Great Lakes Presbytery of the Bible Presbyterian Church, a member of the Home Mission Committee of that denomination, and is on the Board of Directors of the Summer Bible School Association. He is the first regular called pastor of the Covenant Church and has been in Grove City since June 1938. This was his first charge. He says he regrets leaving Grove City, the many friends he has made here, and especially those who have labored so faithfully with him to establish this testimony...At the farewell party the congregation presented Rev. Schaeffer with a gold Elgin watch and Mrs. Schaeffer with a beaten aluminum bowl and platter. The Enterprise Sunday School where Mr. Schaeffer preached monthly, gave him a money gift of ten dollars. Refreshments were served prepared by the ladies of the church...[1]

That summer while Fran and Edith looked for a house in Chester they stayed with the Lairds in Wilmington. They found a four-bedroom house being built. It was beyond their means but Pop Schaeffer loaned them the money for the down payment. Edith was thrilled. She could pick wallpaper and everything that adorned the interior. Fran now drove a used Chevrolet. His Model A had worn out - perhaps from too often carrying 17 boys to wienie roasts! Fran's new church had a congregation of 500. They met in an old mill building. Associate pastor Fran helped 76-year-old pastor Dr. Lathem by preaching Sunday nights, making most of the pastoral calls and ministering to young people. Fran also evangelized among

---

[1] Schaeffer, *Tapestry*, 214.

blue collar workers, a task he was well suited for. Fran could talk their talk.

"I love hearing 'Rev' preach. You can always understand him," was a comment Edith often heard.

The winter was gloomy. Not only was the Nazi dictator Hitler over-running Europe with his 'blitzkrieg' or 'lightning war'', but his ally Japan attacked American naval forces in Hawaii December 7, 1941. The treachery came on a Sunday morning. Edith was playing on the floor with baby Susan and four-year-old Priscilla when the attack was announced on the radio. It sounded like America's entire navy had been destroyed! The next day America was officially at war. But what would they fight with? And how would the Japanese be stopped now? This world war was going to be larger than the first world war.

"'World War II' it is called," said some gloomily.

In the autumn of 1942 regular night-time air raid practices began. Because no lights were allowed outside homes they were called 'blackouts'. Enemy bombers would be attracted to lights. Lights were allowed in the homes if the windows were covered. The tiniest streak of light piercing the outside darkness might bring a helmeted air-raid warden hammering on the door. It was a miserable winter for Edith, made much worse by the two daughters getting chicken pox, whooping cough, and mumps - one after the other! It was heart-breaking to see the girls so sickly and pale all the time. The winter gloom was followed by Pop Schaeffer's death in June 1943. He was in a coma for three days but Fran and Edith were sure he could hear them. They read the Bible, talked to him and prayed with him.

"I'm certain I saw a smile flicker across his lips," said Edith.

Fran's work never stopped. He had to monitor the building plans for the church, because the session was building a stone church in Chester. Of course Fran was very well suited for the job. But it was time-consuming. Many nights Fran worked with the men of the church on their new building - not supervising but hammering, sawing and plumbing! Fran's relationship with the men could not be formal in such circumstances. He formed a close bond to them. But a problem loomed. Fran soon realized the large building they were all pouring their hearts and souls into was not the last. Dr. Lathem wanted to go right on building others. In fact he had a complex in mind. Fran felt it was extravagant.

"I'm very troubled by this," he told Edith. "These people are not well-to-do."

So when Fran was approached in 1943 by the Bible Presbyterian Church in St. Louis, he listened. As busy as he had been he felt like he had been in Chester half his life, not just two years. There seemed nothing that had not happened: war, blackouts, death of a parent, severe illnesses of his children, building a church, endless pastoral calls. He had started a class for children with Down's syndrome. He had even been a street preacher at times. He had once performed a healing! A little girl's doctor had pronounced her tongue disease terminal. The girls' mother had the elders appeal to Fran for help. Edith prepared a vial of oil - cooking oil - for Fran. With the elders Fran went to the girls' bedside.

"Is anyone among you sick?" Fran read James 5:14. "Let them call the elders of the church to pray over them and anoint them with oil in the name of the Lord."

Fran anointed the child's forehead with oil, then placed his hands on her. All the elders placed their hands on her too. They prayed fervently for her recovery, for this 'promise' in the book of James to occur. The girl recovered! Edith was as overjoyed as Fran. How could they ever hope to do more than that in Chester? Certainly people in St. Louis needed ministering just as much as people in Chester. But leaving Chester was painful in many ways.

Once Edith buried her face in a cushion. "Oh, I don't even know how to pray...but God how can we be sure that we are right? What about all these people? Please, please make Your will clear..."

Suddenly she stopped crying. She began to sing:

> My will made known to thee,
> As thou dost wait on me.
> The future now thou canst not see,
> But I will work for thee.
> My will, my will made known to thee,
> As thou dost wait on me,
> my will, my will made known to thee,
> As thou dost wait on Me.[1]

She sang to the melody of Frances Havergal's hymn 'I Gave My Life For Thee'. Edith loved Frances Havergal. But Edith did not remember the verses she had just sung. Curious, she found the 'I

---

[1] Schaeffer, *Tapestry*, 224-5.

Gave My Life For Thee' in a hymn book. The verses she sang did not exist! She was stunned, then awed, certain God had answered her prayer instantly by putting those words on her tongue.

'Yes, do Thy will,' she reflected.

She knew future choices would loom up time and time again, but she was sure now He would make His will known. Still, leaving Chester was painful. She had splurged her tiny inheritance from Aunt Jennie on a playground in the backyard - little of which could be moved. Edith had many bonds in Chester too. She was very close to the Bethel Missionary Band, a dear group of pious ladies. Fran was wrenched too. He visited every family and every individual in the congregation before leaving. He prayed with them one last time, assuring them he would still be accessible. And both Fran and Edith had to leave their parents once again.

Edith's gift from God did not satisfy her for long. She was more and more agitated over the arrangements in St. Louis. They were in the process of leaving for St. Louis when Edith severely burned her face with her new steam iron. Fran rushed her to the hospital. Doctors spread a thick ointment over the second degree burns on her face and wrapped it with gauze. She had three slits in huge mummy-like covering, two for her eyes and one for her mouth. She was sure that she had an experience just like Fran's many years before when they were moving to the Faith Seminary in Wilmington. God had drawn her up short - and chastened her!

"I'm sorry, Lord. I'll stop my struggling against your will, whatever it is…"

St. Louis awed Edith. Near sprawling Forest Park with its superb zoo was their red-brick church - at the corner of Union and Enright. The church was splendid inside: dark wood pews, a pipe organ and a choir loft. Walls were dark panels with stained glass windows. Massive beams skied upward to arch into the ceiling high above. They located a house on Waterman Boulevard - within walking distance of the zoo. The house seemed better than a dream. Thirteen rooms! The three-story house had bay windows, a fireplace with built-in bookcases on both sides, a sun room for reading and sewing, and a study on the third floor for Fran - everything!

"This could be the place," gushed Edith, "where we are to have a family homestead, the things I've wanted ever since coming to America from China."[1]

---

[1] Schaeffer, *Tapestry*, 231.

Priscilla walked to Hamilton grade school. Susan was not yet three. Fran plunged into his Sunday routine of preaching sermons morning and evening, and ministering a late afternoon youth meeting. On Wednesday evening he ministered a prayer meeting, followed by Bible study. Of course he also had meetings with the Sunday School Board and various committees. And he could not neglect attempts to evangelize the unchurched. He was so busy he had only one significant period of free time: Monday afternoon.

Edith began using their home - with its ample room - for church activities. In the basement she held a class for small pre-school children, quickly attracting children of every religious bent: Jewish, Catholic, Protestant and unchurched. Once a week at home Fran instructed volunteers how to teach children the Bible. Later 20 of these volunteers would hold classes in their own homes. Most of the 'Bible study' was fun activity. Fran and Edith both became very earnest in their ministry to children.

"It is so important to instruct them early," they emphasized.

The very first year in St. Louis Fran and Edith expanded their program into 'Seven Points How", which would later be called 'Children for Christ'. Bible classes in homes were point one of the program. Each child would get a 'Children for Christ' certificate and a pin shaped like a fish. There were also awards children love to earn. Point two, 'Released Time Classes', took advantage of state programs that released pupils from school for voluntary religious teaching one hour a week. Point three, 'open air work', was for children to meet in parks or on beaches to have fun in Christian activities. Point four was 'Empire Builder Clubs' for boys and girls. These were similar to scouting but with greater Christian emphasis. Fran wrote a manual similar to the scout manual. Point five was the Schaeffers' well-polished Summer Bible School. Point six was a summer camp program, at which the Schaeffers were also very experienced. Camp would follow the Bible School. Point seven was to be a large, annual city-wide rally to showcase what the children had learned as well as encourage them to continue. Edith was as nervous about the first annual rally as she had been about the first summer Bible class they had initiated back in Grove City.

"How many children will come?" she fretted.

The first rally was to be held in the church. Edith had worked hard at making props for the rally. The theme was Noah and the flood. She made large silhouettes in cardboard of Noah, his family, the ark and the animals! She had made a screen behind which

72

volunteers moved the cardboard figures. As the rally began she watched with apprehension, then wonder as more and more clamoring children arrived, most with their parents.

"I estimate 700 kids," said Fran.

Noah and the flood went flawlessly. The climax of the evening to Edith was the singing of 'When the Saints Come Marching In'. A helper plunked the piano with fire as Edith led the singing. Edith got goose bumps as 700 high-pitched voices joined her. Did these budding Christians see Christ and his saints returning in glory as she did? She was still thrilled later as Fran ended the rally by reading off the names of those children who had distinguished themselves. The Sunday edition of the *St. Louis Post Dispatch* had complete coverage of the rally with many photographs. The text of the article praised the rally. Edith was so thrilled she was already planning next years rally.

"I'm planning Jonah and the whale!"

Children for Christ spread to other denominations and other geographic locations. But Fran restricted it to churches belonging to the American Council for Christian Churches. Carl McIntire spearheaded the founding of the ACCC in 1941. It was in response to the older National Council of Evangelicals, which presumed to speak for all Evangelicals, but also in response to the much older Federal Council of Churches, which presumed to speak for all Protestants. Membership in ACCC was not large but it was 'pure', with only denominations that believed in the inerrancy of the Bible and opposed modernism.

Fran muttered, "I'll not allow our careful, accurate exposition of the Bible for children to be ripped apart by modernists."

Because Fran became increasingly more active in the ACCC the life of the Schaeffers was busy every waking minute. Fran seldom had an evening free. Edith's evenings were not free either. She had to care for the children, as well as keep up on the laundry and housework. When Fran returned home Edith ate with him by the fireplace or on the patio. Edith's time with him alone usually started at midnight! They both were indeed married to Christ. The future looked to be the same.

Monday afternoon, Fran's only free time during the day, was for family outings. Often in winter they went to the Art Museum. The girls carried art paper, pencils, charcoal, and pastels. At some point they would sit and sketch a painting or perhaps a fountain in the courtyard while Fran and Edith strolled leisurely through exhibits.

In warm weather they went on picnics or visited the zoo. They stayed at home on occasion to play games or have a 'treasure hunt' meal in which the girls had to search for their hot dogs or slices of watermelon. But staying home was risky. Fran or Edith could be snagged by a church 'problem' at any moment.

The Schaeffers had many Jewish neighbors. Because of Hitler's assault on Jews Fran felt it was time for the Bible Presbyterian Church to take a more visible stand. So he wrote the tract 'The Bible-believing Christian and the Jew', which his church distributed by the thousands. He ended its message with a poem he had heard once in New York City:

> How odd of God to choose the Jew,
> But not so odd as those who choose
> The Jewish God and hate the Jew.

In the fall of 1944 Edith was pregnant again. The year 1945 promised many great joys. The outcome of World War II had become obvious by end of June 1944. Italian Fascists had already surrendered. But the German Fascists had to be defeated. That month Americans and British successfully invaded Nazi-occupied Europe. The German air force was virtually destroyed. The Americans and British were pushing back the Germans from the west. The Russians were pushing back the Germans from the east. That same month of June in the Pacific the Americans virtually destroyed all of Japan's aircraft carriers.

In May 1945 a very pregnant Edith volunteered their home for a wedding. She cleaned the house top to bottom and even prepared 'ribbon sandwiches' of cream cheese colored green and pink. In addition she made cream puff shells filled with chicken salad. By the time the ceremony started she was so frazzled and large with child she could not attend! Within hours Fran had to rush her to the hospital. Edith experienced yet another method of childbirth, this time in a state called 'twilight sleep'. To her horror she found out later that although she had no memory of the event she was 'conscious', ranting and raving though the entire labor and birth. She had even bitten her own hands!

'Who could have devised such a diabolical procedure?' she fumed, feeling her cuts and bruises.

But she was salved by the sight of her daughter, Deborah, who had been born after 12 hours of labor on May 3. 'The third daughter of the third daughter,' she reflected. On August 6, 1945, the world was shocked by the first atomic bomb. No ordinary person had an inkling such a weapon existed. One bomb leveled Hiroshima, a large city in northern Japan. But fanatical Japanese still would not surrender, perhaps thinking only one such bomb existed. But on August 9 a second bomb leveled the Japanese city of Nagasaki.

On the night of August 14 people flooded the streets of St. Louis, screaming, "The war is over, the war is over."

America would change with an influx of millions of young men and women released from armed service. Life would be busier than ever for a pastor and his family. As if Fran didn't have enough to do he also became active in the Independent Board for Presbyterian Foreign Missions and had to go to Philadelphia for meetings. This stirred up old feelings in both Fran and Edith of wanting to 'go forth' as missionaries. They framed pictures from *Asia* magazine: a fisherman casting his nets, a tall dignified woman carrying a load on her head, rice fields, small boats. Edith made a sign: 'Go ye into all the world...' Would God ever call them to go forth?

One day Fran said, "Edith, if the Lord opened the way for me to study further - say in Scotland - would you be willing for all the difficulties that would bring, with three children?"

"Yes, of course...," she gasped.

What did Fran know that she didn't know? At their spring 1947 meeting, the Independent Board of Presbyterian Foreign Missions discussed the state of Europe after the devastating world war. The liberal churches were rushing in to help. Where were conservative churches? Wouldn't Fran's Children for Christ work in Europe? Almost magically Fran was picked to survey the situation. He was to go to Europe for three months! His session in St. Louis consented.

Elmer and Jane Smick came to live in the Schaeffer home and take over their work. The Schaeffers headed east. Edith went to Brewster, Massachusetts, where she and the three girls lived with her sister Janet and her two boys, eight and two. Edith and Janet had no transportation but regularly walked the children two miles to the beach. Edith relished her time in Brewster. At 41 and almost nine years older, Janet was the sister whom Edith scarcely knew. Now Edith finally got to know her well. They were joined for two weeks by Elsa, now 39, and her two young daughters, six and three.

Edith knew this summer was a very special gift. "Praise God for this precious time with my sisters."

Meanwhile Fran toured Europe!

Chapter 10

"Geneva!" gushed Fran.

On July 16, 1947, Fran visited that city of over 100,000 in the western end of Switzerland. It was hallowed ground for a Reformed church member. It was the city of John Calvin. The great Reformer had arrived there in 1536 a distinguished 27-year-old Protestant scholar from France. Older Reformer William Farel had already converted Geneva. Calvin wanted a quiet scholarly life. But William Farel bullied him into becoming an activist. So Calvin matured both as an activist and as a scholar. More than any other Reformer he articulated the principles of Protestantism. His writing was brilliant, structured and persuasive. Although the first revolutionary had been Luther and the second Zwingli, it was Calvin's theology that swept western Europe and eventually America.

'The four great Reformers,' thought Fran as he gazed at the Reformation Monument.

There in stone stood William Farel, John Calvin, Theodore Beza and John Knox. Beza had been Calvin's assistant and successor. John Knox founded Presbyterianism in Scotland after spending time with Calvin in Geneva. Fran could hardly believe he stood in the center of the Reformed movement. He liked everything about Switzerland. The air was sweet. Food was plentiful and cheap.

Fran went to Europe an innocent. He had almost no contacts, no names. He prayed God would take him to people in sympathy with the Bible. In Europe he met 'Christian' leaders of all stripes. He developed a sense of his heritage from the Reformation, as well as a sense of urgency over its future. European churches were much more liberal than American churches. Of 60 pastors in the Geneva State Church, only three at most believed the Bible! The liberals had virtually declared war on conservative Bible-believing churches. Fran was sickened to hear a leading liberal in Norway scream at youths to confront Bible-believing Christians and "drive the grayheads out!"[1] It was time, the liberal ranted, for the church to be a social organ for progress. Liberals merely wanted the church as an instrument to further liberal social agendas.

---

[1] Louis G. Parkhurst, Jr., *Francis Schaeffer: the Man and His Work*. (Wheaton, Ill.: Tyndale House Publishers, 1985), 68.

"Oh, how I long for some Christian contact," he muttered after attending one of these liberal gatherings.

In America, theologian Reinhold Neibuhr spoke the same social message. These liberals were forming the World Council of Churches. To accommodate one and all the WCC was willing to water down Christianity until only a non-spiritual socialist agenda was left. Bible-believing Christians had to counter the WCC with an international organization of their own. By the time Fran had left Europe he had many contacts who also desired an international organization of Bible-believers. He received numerous requests to come back to help the beleaguered Bible-believers of Europe.

He was more convinced than ever that Bible-believers must separate themselves from the liberals, who were only nominal Christians. He opposed the so-called 'Ecumenical Movement'. It was deadly to Christianity in his opinion. Later he would write:

> Nowhere is practicing the truth more important than in the area of religious cooperation... if... I am willing publicly to act as though that man's religious position [which is contrary to the Word of God] is the same as my own, I have destroyed the practice of truth which my generation can expect from me and which it will demand of me if I am to have credibility...[1]

His organization in America was well prepared for his return. The letters he wrote Edith from Europe she had carefully recopied for publication within the church. Fran came back to report to both the Independent Board of Presbyterian Foreign Missions and to the American Council of Christian Churches. They were alarmed - but pleased with his work. How he relished getting back to St. Louis. Ministering a congregation was exhausting but not as agitating and stressful as confronting the enemy. He hoped he wouldn't have to travel again for weeks, maybe months. But he did not at all expect what soon happened.

"The Independent Board of Presbyterian Foreign Missions wants us to be missionaries to Europe!" he told Edith.

"Europe!"

---

[1] Francis A. Schaeffer, *Two Contents, Two Realities*. (Downers Grove, Ill.: InterVarsity Press, 1974) in Schaeffer, Francis, *The Complete Works of Francis A. Schaeffer: a Christian Worldview*, v. 4. (Westchester, Illinois : Crossway Books, 1982), 281.

The position had a short fuse too. The Bible-believing churches had indeed gathered forces to create the International Council of Christian Churches. Its first meeting would be held in Amsterdam in August 1948. The missionaries had to be there before that date. In fact they wanted Fran - should he accept - to be there in February 1948! This would be a hazardous mission. This missionary would become a very visible opponent to modernism. He would be greatly outnumbered. But what choice did Fran have? Hadn't he led the Bible-believing churches in Europe to believe help would arrive from America? Hadn't he told their American counterparts the situation was grim.

"How can we now refuse to go?" he asked Edith.

"We can't."

"We can work out of Switzerland."

While visiting their families one last time in Germantown the Schaeffers had Priscilla tested at Philadelphia Children's Hospital. She had been suffering waves of nausea for months. During some tests in the hospital she was noticed by the tall, imposing surgeon-in-chief of the hospital. He was allowed to examine her. 'Mesenteric endenitis,' he concluded. Within one day he had removed her appendix and she was recovering. The Schaeffers were very impressed by the surgeon-in-chief. And he said he was very impressed by the overt way the Schaeffers lived their Christianity.

"I just became a Christian a couple of weeks ago," the surgeon-in-chief confided to Edith.[1]

His name was C. Everett Koop.

Edith was sure their paths had crossed as part of God's plan. Who knew what might have happened had Priscilla gone to Europe with her problem not diagnosed correctly? In August 1948 the cruise in the *Nieuw Amsterdam* across the Atlantic was not as relaxing as Edith had hoped. It was not Priscilla who was sick on the ship but Susan. Finally the ship entered Holland through a long channel, passing mile after mile of green lowlands dotted with windmills and cattle. The Dutch were not blasé at the sight of the huge ocean liner but gawked out their windows and waved. Edith warmed at the sight. Weren't these Dutch the very ones they had come to save?

Small boats full of tourists tooted their shrill horns and the ocean liner boomed its deep rumbly answer. The Schaeffers disembarked

---

[1] Schaeffer, *Tapestry*, 281.

in Rotterdam. Fran was apprehensive about going through Dutch customs. They had a sizeable cargo: 17 pieces of luggage, several crates, four bicycles and a refrigerator! What if the customs official wanted to open everything? The official scanned the cargo. He asked crisply if they had any tobacco or liquor.

"No," answered Edith.

A couple more questions and they were through customs. Not one item opened! What a good sign from God. They stored the bulk of their belongings in Rotterdam and took the rest, including their bicycles, to the ocean resort town of Scheveningen. The beaches were crowded. 'Gaudy' was Edith's opinion of the outdoor cafes, ice-cream stores, fish stands and bright lights that tracked the beach. Fortunately the house where they stayed was away from the beach. But it was next to the terminal for the tram line into Scheveningen. Chattery people flowed in and out of the resort night and day.

Sunday morning they improvised Sunday School for the girls and a Dutch boy staying in the house. The next day Fran left for Amsterdam to help set the stage for the conference. Edith noted the ease with which he got around Holland. He had 'learned the ropes' very well. Meanwhile Edith and the girls experienced the diet of a Dutch family. Breakfast was milk with bread, butter and jam. The dark bread was moist and heavy. Lunch was bread, butter, and one thin slice of cheese or lunch meat. Supper was soup of potatoes and cauliflower or string beans, plus either fish or cheese. Dessert was sour cream or cornstarch pudding. Luckily milk was always available and in quantity. The girls began to crave things that they had disdained before.

"No eggs for breakfast?" they asked before long.

Edith was struck by the fact that although she was in an exotic foreign land she spent most of her time trying to improvise. She had to wash clothes in a sink that ran only cold water. She had to iron on a table covered with Debby's blanket. Yet she managed to do all of that, as well as write letters. Moreover, she was also working her way though shorthand and typing lessons so she could help Fran as his secretary. She wanted to finish the lessons before they settled in Switzerland because there they all would be taking French lessons! On Sunday all the Schaeffers took a taxi to The Hague and visited a minister in his home. He smoked black cigars almost constantly, as most Dutch men did. Edith was stunned when the minister's family shared their weekly ration of meat. Fran's piece - the largest - was a one-inch square! The main dish was potatoes and string beans. Edith and Fran were aghast to learn how much tea the Dutch drank.

"When I make my afternoon calls I drink about 20 cups of tea," said the minister.

During the conference in Amsterdam Edith attended almost as often as Fran. Their host family in Scheveningen was happy to watch the children. Priscilla at 11 was quite the little mother anyway. The trip to the conference - tram from Scheveningen to Den Haag, then train for The Hague, then tram to Amsterdam - took two hours. In Amsterdam Edith slipped into a back pew inside the ancient 'Beginjhof'. This was the same building in which Pilgrims knelt to pray before sailing to America! Arie Kok, Holland's ambassador to China, gave the opening speech. Kok said their stand for God's Word against the liberals and the world was like Gideon and his band standing against the Midianites.

Later in the week Edith brought the three girls into Amsterdam so they could hear Fran deliver his speech. Of course to be in Amsterdam and not visit the art in the Rijksmuseum would have been gross negligence. So Edith took the girls to see the 'Dutch masters', highlighted by Rembrandt, as well as more recent masters like Vincent van Gogh. Once Fran came back to Scheveningen fuming. Kok had tried to coerce the Independent Board into loaning Fran to the ICCC. This would have put their move to Switzerland on ice. Fran spoke strongly against it. He was sure the Lord had led him to do missionary work. In fact, he would not serve the ICCC! And he stormed out of the meeting.

"I guess I still have a bit of a temper," Fran admitted.

During the conference Fran met Hans Rookmaaker, an art historian. Hans had heard Fran preach and approached him. Fran, very busy, allowed Hans half an hour. They both astonished each other. Fran had never met an art critic who was also a studious Bible-believing Christian. Hans had never met a Bible-believing Christian minister who knew so much about art. For Fran had been visiting art galleries in Europe at every opportunity and typical of all his interests he delved deeply into art and its meaning. Fran and Hans were oblivious of the time as they happily discussed the relationship of art to Christianity through the centuries. Fran's 'half hour' became a mutual joke. At that first meeting they had talked until four o'clock in the morning!

"We've barely scratched the surface," concluded Fran, "but I'm certain God wants us to meet again."

Near the end of the Schaeffers' stay in Holland the Dutch began decorating streets with their incomparable flowers for coronation of a new queen. Bad health had caused Queen Wilhelmina to abdicate. Daughter Juliana was crowned September 6. It seemed all Holland was ablaze with color. It made a splendid last memory of Holland, for the Schaeffers left the next day. After side trips to Belgium and France they arrived by train in Lausanne, Switzerland.

The smell of the air was so pure and clean. Shimmering to the south of Lausanne was Lake Geneva, also called Lac Léman. The largest lake in central Europe, it was only five to ten miles wide but 45 miles long. The lake was said to be 1000 feet deep. Jutting up on its south side were the Alps. The north was bordered by the foothills of the Jura Mountains. Lausanne itself - a city of well over 100,000 - was all hills. As their taxi chugged ever higher to their lodging it seemed all of Lausanne was below them. At 'Riant Mont' the Schaeffers were greeted by Madame Turian and her two young maids. Madam Turian's 'pension', or boarding house, backed into the hillside. A stone wall kept 'the front yard from falling into the street', in Edith's mind.[1] First, they had to climb up the front yard to the house, then huff up stairs to the third floor. There the Schaeffers had two small bedrooms. This would be their home for a time. It was hard to imagine where they would stow all their belongings.

"Each room has an outside balcony," said Edith, trying to remain cheerful.

But it was a cheery place. Cow bells tinkled from the fields beyond. The girls could play in the front yard on clearings under pine and fruit trees. Fruit trees were pruned so that they grew branches only from two sides. That way they were grown right up against a wall or fence. In some yards a row of trees formed a fence. Madame Turian's front yard also was lush with flowers: dahlias, chrysanthemums, daisies and roses. The back yard not only had a vegetable garden but a small house for chickens and rabbits too. Priscilla was deemed old enough to collect the daily handful of eggs.

The Schaeffers hired a French tutor, Madame Wildermuth, and soon all the Schaeffers feverishly studied French. Edith had a head start, having studied French in high school. Fran and Edith quickly found a school for the children, including three-year-old Debby, that was a 15-minute walk from the pension. The family arose at 7

---

[1] Edith Schaeffer, *With Love, Edith: The L'Abri Family Letters, 1948-1960*. (San Francisco: Harper & Row, 1988), 35.

AM, ate oatmeal and toast, then went at their various activities - the girls to school, Fran and Edith either sharing Fran's work or studying French. Madam Turian's lunch was potatoes, plus fish or meat or cheese, and spinach, beets, carrots, or onions. 'Dessert' at lunch was an apple or a pear. Dinner began with porridge, followed by rice or pasta and cheese or meat depending on the particular day of the week. Sunday was always rabbit, Wednesday, cheese, Friday, fish, and so on. The Schaeffers delayed house-hunting until they knew the language and the country better. Meanwhile, the children battled a succession of minor illnesses. Debby had bronchitis.

A woman doctor who specialized in chest ailments came to the pension, examined Debby and said in fractured English, "She wishes to have pneumonia..."[1]

With medicine pneumonia was averted.

Soon the Schaeffers received their permit to stay in Lausanne. But it carried an ominous warning: *No evangelization in Suisse.* They could not evangelize in Switzerland! Fran and Edith looked at each other and shrugged. God would change that edict if it was His will. Meanwhile they couldn't evangelize anyway until they learned the language. In their rooms Fran conducted a Sunday service for the five of them, preaching to them just as he would have to 5000.

Sometimes Edith wondered if they had not taken a step backward. When winter came the air was icy. Even though their pension had a furnace that circulated hot water through radiators the Schaeffers had to dress as warmly as possible. Lighting in the evenings was dismal, with anything more than one 20-watt bulb frowned on. Electricity was precious. Edith was worried more for Priscilla and Susan than anyone else. The 11-year-old and 7-year-old had been suddenly thrust into schools where only French was spoken. The school allowed them to study only mathematics and French until their language was proficient enough to move into other subjects. Edith spared them French in the pension.

"You may knit or start stamp collections," she told them.

The Schaeffers did not neglect exercise. They often bicycled. In spite of that precaution Fran had a scare. His left shoulder and chest began to ache. He had no energy. He was sure it was a heart attack. He was only 36! But their woman doctor assured him it was neuralgia, caused by lack of sleep. She injected him with vitamins

---

[1] Schaeffer, *With Love, Edith,* 42.

and calcium and ordered him to rest. He doubted the doctor but her diagnosis turned out to be correct. Soon he felt fine.

They celebrated Christmas of 1948 with residents of the pension over a turkey dinner. Priscilla surprised everyone by reciting a Christmas poem in French. After Christmas they took the train to Bern, then to Spiez on Lac Thun. From there they ascended into the rugged Swiss Alps to Adelboden where they stayed at Pension Hari. They were just a few miles from the great peak Jungfrau. What a spot to begin skiing! But they did for two days - even tiny Debby. When they returned to Lausanne they sensed the irony.

"This strange foreign place now seems home," they all agreed.

In early 1949 Fran was told by a retired Swiss minister and his friend on the police force that the restriction on evangelizing was contrary to the Swiss constitution. They enlisted a lawyer to write the authorities a sharp letter. All the Schaeffers could do is wait and look for a house. But house-hunting was discouraging, with most available houses too expensive and unfurnished at that. Priscilla continued to improve in school, even getting 100 percent on one of her many dictation tests. Her younger sisters were catching up with their classmates even faster.

Madame Wildermuth, Fran and Edith's French tutor, was raised in Champery, a Swiss mountain village. Every summer Madame Wildermuth and her relatives lived there in a chalet for two months. She asked if the Schaeffers would be interested in renting a chalet in Champery for the summer. They could continue their French lessons and the children would love the mountains. Madame Turian said it would be no problem. She could easily rent their two rooms for the summer, then let them return in the fall.

"Would you mind checking it out, Edith?" Fran asked. "I'll stay with the children."

So Edith rode the train along the north flank of the great lake to Montreux, then on to Aigle on the Rhone River. From there a two-car train chugged up 20 miles into the mountains to Champery. There Madame Wildermuth was waiting to show Edith around the charming village. Up a steep winding path - but not as high as Madame Wildermuth's own chalet - was a furnished chalet available for the summer. A chalet by definition was an all-wood house with balconies facing the south. But that couldn't describe the wonderful feeling the chalet gave Edith. She arranged to rent it and returned to Lausanne with the good news.

In Lausanne was even more good news...

Chapter 11

"The authorities have relented," announced Fran happily.

Now Fran and Edith could speak in public and hold 'small' meetings, although any large meetings would have to be approved by the authorities first. Meanwhile Fran had been attending activities held by Mr. Andre of the Brethren. Mr. Andre was already doing much of what Fran intended to do. He ministered successfully to local children. So Fran was sure he could serve many children who needed Christ. As well as adults. Edith never missed a chance now to discuss worship, especially with young women. She was much more likely than Fran to approach someone in public. Some were put off by her boldness but many were receptive. She often used what the family called the 'Gospel walnut'. A gift of the American Missionary Alliance, it was hollow with ribbon wound around an axle inside. A tiny metal crank turned the axle.

The first three inches of the ribbon was black. "This is your sin," Edith informed her startled listener.

The next three inches were red. "This is the Savior's blood."

Then she pulled the ribbon out farther until it turned white. "Jesus died to wash your sins away."

The walnut seemed simple-minded, yet many people did not understand even that much about Christianity. In March Fran was delighted to hear from a couple in Holland who wanted to start Children for Christ programs. They appealed to Fran and Edith to come during the month of April to help them get started. How could the Schaeffers refuse? Before they left however Mr. Andre invited Fran, now unfettered, to speak to the Brethren. Forty people listened to Fran expound on how modernism was not only ruining the modern church but was offering people only confusion and despair. He stressed how important Children for Christ programs were. The children had to be reached before they were hopelessly confused. His listeners, maybe expecting a travelog on America, were stunned by the urgency in Fran's message. Mr. Andre was so impressed he offered to immediately begin translating Fran's memory packets for children from English into French!

"Everywhere I feel more and more the thirst for the real Christ in people," Fran told Edith. "They can not articulate their despair until

I explain what has happened to their church. Could that become my mission someday?"

Then they and the children too were off to Holland. The children would miss little school because spring vacation ran for three weeks. In Holland Fran presented his Children for Christ program to ministers from five churches. Reassured of the program's integrity they allowed him to make his presentation to the five congregations. Many volunteers were needed. And Fran and Edith had to prepare those volunteers to teach the classes. Fran's teaching material had to be translated into Dutch. Volunteering for this task was the art historian Hans Rookmaaker and his wife Anky. Once again Hans and Fran discussed art and Christianity at every opportunity. But Fran had many speaking engagements: to youth groups of the churches, to the Christian Reformed Students' League, and even to a meeting of seamen.

Over the next months Mr. Kok of the ICCC, grateful for Fran's continued help to the organization, also campaigned for the Children for Christ programs. Inquiries about the program began to come in to Fran from all over Europe. Meanwhile the Schaeffers moved to the mountains and Champery for the summer. Champery was so delightful Edith thought about living there year around. She adored mountain life. Fran assured her it was impractical. As if to prove it he got lost in the mountains one day while hiking in a very steep area with Priscilla and Susan. They had an inglorious descent.

"We had to crawl down a dry streambed - when we weren't sliding out of control," grumbled the dusty girls.

On September 17, 1949, the Schaeffers celebrated the first anniversary of arriving in Switzerland. Out of the blue, while Fran was on a trip, their landlady in Champery talked to Edith about renting a chalet in Champery year around. She said the rent in the non-summer months was much cheaper. In fact the total for the rest of the year was about the same as the total for the summer! Edith was amazed. It was much cheaper than Lausanne and so much roomier. Her mind jumped ahead. They still had the refrigerator and other things in storage too. Now they could get them out. Why couldn't they make Champery their home? She had to consider every angle though. Fran was a stickler. How much more would it cost Fran to travel? What about the girls' education? How cold was it during the winter? On and on she raised questions, then got answers. When Fran returned she flooded him with facts.

Backpedaling he said, "If it is a saving in money, if it is workable for our work, if the children can get schooling here, and if it will be better for their health - if we find all this to be true..."[1]

Suddenly Edith's dream was reality. Priscilla at 12 would have to go to Ecole Alpina, a private school away from Champery. But the same would have been true in Lausanne. They rented Chalet des Frenes, which had been built by an English woman 20 years before. After living in Madame Turian's pension Edith was ecstatic. The property had a large yard and the chalet had - almost unheard of for Champery - central heating. Inside was wood paneling painted white and wood floors covered with rugs. Living room, dining room and kitchen made up the first floor. Five bedrooms made up the second floor. The third floor had two more rooms and a large storage area. The chalet was so spacious it immediately made the Schaeffers realize it could even be used in their ministry. More and more they encountered students wandering aimlessly through Europe. These students, usually depressed, were searching for something the modern age did not provide. Could the Schaeffers now shelter searchers like these and counsel them?

'Yet how would they even know that we are here, up in this isolated village?' wondered Edith.

Happily, the Schaeffer girls were even more eager than Edith to stay in Champery. And this time the authorities issued permits with no restrictions about evangelizing. It seemed providence. They had their possessions they had stored for two years: refrigerator, barrel of dishes, box of kitchen utensils, lamps, pictures, knickknacks, books and the children's double-decker bed. When they had packed those things two years before in St. Louis the children had known no French. Now Susan and Debby spoke French as their first language! Priscilla was not far behind. On November 18 Champery had its first heavy snowfall of the winter. Nevertheless the Schaeffers got about when they had to. Shortly after that heavy snow, Edith went with Fran to Paris for one of his ICCC meetings.

"The future looks very busy," they agreed.

As if Fran did not have enough to do he began preparing Bible lessons to help older, faltering Christians who wanted to get back in touch with their beliefs. This effort had been triggered by a doctor who was curious about the Bible but was overwhelmed by the challenge. So Fran wrote *Basic Bible Studies*. He dictated each study

---

[1] Schaeffer, *With Love, Edith*, 99.

to Edith, who typed it with multiple carbon copies. These were passed out. Then Edith would type more copies.

Fran traveled to Scandinavia in the spring of 1950. The Free Lutheran Church of Norway, among others, wanted him to show them how to set up Children for Christ programs. During 1950 the Chalet des Frenes hosted many church people who were going to attend the Second Plenary Congress of the International Council of Christian Churches to be held in August. Before the conference Fran had the opportunity to meet the 64-year-old Swiss theologian who was the darling of non-believers. Karl Barth, a Reformed minister no less, revolted Fran. Barth was saying now as a theologian what earlier had been said only by secular philosophers.

"Did God create the world?" Fran asked Barth point blank.

"God created the world in the first century A. D.," answered Barth.

"This world?" asked Fran, waving at the forest outside.

"This world does not matter," answered Barth.[1]

So Fran had his answer. Barth had separated the physical world from the spiritual world into two unconnected realities. The creation in Genesis was completely irrelevant to Barth. No wonder non-believing intelligentsia admired Barth. He had separated faith from their world. Barth's movement was called the oxymoron 'Neo-orthodoxy'. Fran developed his conversation into a talk titled 'The New Modernism (Neo-orthodoxy) and the Bible.' for the coming Congress . He hoped to later publish it as an article.

Fran remained just as feisty as he ever was, warning in talks that Bible-believing Christians must not compromise with modernism nor lose heart and withdraw. If they withdrew who would spread the Gospel? Yet the battle corrupted some. He warned also against becoming hard-hearted. Bible-believing Christians must produce scholarly, rigorous work but they must not neglect warm devotional material either. Fran worried that some Bible-believing people involved in the battle for truth were losing the love God commands all to have for one another. Some in his own movement showed hostility and rancor.

Fran also told Edith, "I'm very worried about some of us becoming obsessed with winning rather than with being right."

In 1950 American soldiers still occupied much of Germany. Fran and Edith went to a base near Munich to teach a two-week Vacation

[1] Michael S. Hamilton, *Christianity Today*, March 3, 1997, 24.

Bible School for the children of American soldiers. The Schaeffers made a good impression on American army personnel. The best proof of the effectiveness of the Bible School was the children who attended. They had become knowledgeable about the Bible. The American army had an enormous presence in Europe. Fran soon had other requests from the army for his Bible study programs.

Europe was a constant education for Fran too. Just outside Munich was Dachau, the site of a Nazi concentration camp. Dachau was often called a 'death camp', implying it was a Nazi extermination camp like Auschwitz. In fact Dachau was both a 'work camp' and a 'death camp'. Those less able to work - especially the very youngest and the most elderly - were gassed and incinerated. The more able inmates labored for the Nazi war machine. However, because of the poor diet and living conditions those inmates were usually worked to death. Then they too were incinerated. To make the Dachau camp even more ghastly the Nazis experimented medically with inmates.

'The Nazis at Dachau demonstrate only too horrifically,' observed Fran, 'how some fallen can slither into total abomination.'

In November 1950 Fran went to Rome to observe the Vatican's official recognition of 'The Assumption of the Blessed Virgin Mary' as dogma of the Catholic church. This was the first dogma proclaimed by the church since 1870 when it proclaimed the 'infallibility of the pope'. 'The Assumption of the Blessed Virgin Mary' declared that Mary had been taken up body and soul into heaven. It was just another reminder to Fran that Catholics had over-ridden the Bible with hundreds of years of man-made traditions. It also reinforced the suspicion of many Bible-believers that Catholics worshipped Mary as some kind of minor deity. Certainly the Assumption would make it even harder to ever reconcile Protestants and Catholics, as the ecumenical movement desired. A side product of his trip to Rome was the opportunity for Fran to see more great art.

"Michelangelo, Raphael and Bernini everywhere."

In spite of apparent successes Fran began in 1951 to doubt his own beliefs. Where were the fruits of the Spirit? First of all, in his Bible-believing colleagues he saw little evidence of what the Bible said should be the results or 'fruits' of belief. Instead of 'love, joy, peace, patience, kindness, goodness, faithfulness, gentleness and self-control' promised by Paul in Galatians 5 Fran saw only contention, anger and even hate. And these same fruits, which Fran thought he himself had possessed in abundance years ago after first becoming a Christian, he no longer felt. And yes, he too was full of anger. Where was love? Peace? Patience? Self-control?

"And where is joy?"

In April 1951 he wrote a calm, reasoned letter to a friend:

> ...over Easter, I went to Geneva to...Hugh E. Alexander's Easter Conference...While there, the Lord really spoke to my heart. I had never heard anyone talk and sing about the combat the way those people did. And yet at the same time there was such a spiritual emphasis on the dependence upon the leading of the Holy Spirit, identification with Christ, the need of dying to serve the Lord, and so on and so on, that since being there I felt the burden lifted away. Not that I think the problem is less, but for the first time I see the basic answer. It is the thing for which I have been groping, I think. It is not less combat, but a balance between it and a real following the leading of the Holy Spirit - in short, a care that we do not minimize our personal spiritual lives.
>
> I really feel lighter than I have for years. I do not know what this all means in my relationship to the movement, but I have come to this conclusion - that, God willing, I do not want to lose this joy I have before the Lord. There is nothing that would be worth getting back into the black humor I have been in...[1]

Just days later he had to write the same friend:

> ...My mind is not at rest by any means about all the problems I raised in my last letter to you. I do think that our movement will never be what it could be under the Lord unless the leadership learns to be quiet in the presence of God. It does seem to me that there is a constant tendency to smooth over problems and to the loss not of the weak men, but the stronger ones - perhaps not the loss physically, but the loss as far as leadership is concerned.
>
> I am more and more realizing that Scripturally none of us are ready for leadership until we come to the place before the Lord where we are really ready for His will - regardless of what it is - and therefore, of ourselves, we would prefer not

---

[1] Lane T. Dennis, *Letters of Francis A. Schaeffer*. (Westchester, Ill.: Crossway Books, 1985), 32-3.

to have the leadership, or at least be neutral concerning it. It is out of such stuff that true Christian leadership can come...[1]

The fact that none of his colleagues in the separationist movement had written any real heartfelt literature bothered Fran. He was more and more tuned into art. Then he made a radical decision. Edith was not at all pleased to hear Fran was so troubled he was going to go back to the very beginning and *rethink all his beliefs*. Their entire life was built on belief. She was not troubled by doubt, at least at this point in her life. But now Fran - at the age of 40 - was going to return to being an agnostic!

Day after day almost without pause he thought and brooded. Perhaps his youthful conversion to Christianity was not based on clear thinking. He paced the floors in anguish. Often he had to remove himself from the chalet and walk up into the mountains. After two months he had done more than retrace his steps. He had taken a more mature, a more logical, a more critical journey. But the result was the same. *Only the Bible explained the why and the purpose of mankind.* And yet he still lacked the fruits of the Spirit.

Then at last he thought he saw the answer. "Accepting Christian reality is not enough. That is only a first step. I must study the Bible to understand what it means to live as a Christian." He was not referring to a second act of grace or anything like it. It was more like a holiness attitude. How does one conduct himself as a Christian?

In late 1951 he wrote another friend:

> ...in the past there has been a fallacy in my thinking. That fallacy is simply this: that insofar as we are so abundantly right (as we are concerning the Biblical position of separation), therefore it would certainly follow of a necessity that God's rich blessing would rest upon us as individuals and as a movement. I no longer believe this is so. For increasingly the realization has welled up in my own soul that although this principle [of separation] is of tremendous importance, nevertheless there are other principles in the Word of God which must be kept with equal fidelity if God's full blessing is to be upon us...
>
> What does all this mean to me? I am not sure...[2]

---

[1] Dennis, *Letters of Francis A. Schaeffer*, 34.
[2] Dennis, *Letters of Francis A. Schaeffer*, 35.

In late 1951 he was still writing friends of his inner turmoil and his increasing diminution both in space and in time:

> As it is with space, it is also true of time...time has come to mean something different to me than it ever did before, when time was measured only by the short scope of the hurrying clock or cold dates on a page of the history book. But as time falls into its proper place, again God seems to grow greater by comparison, and again it has the opposite effect on man...
>
> ...If God will spare me, I will have more time yet ahead than has already passed me since I came to mature thinking. But it does not seem to stretch forever as it did even when I first came to Europe four years ago. The three and a half years since I came to Europe have been the most profitable in my life, with only one possible competitor, my three years in seminary. But certainly (with that one possible exception) no period even three times as long has marked me so.
>
> ...Gradually my thinking has changed - I have realized that in many things previously I have been mistaken. When I first found Christ through my Bible reading He was very real to me, and I yet remember the loving wonder of His closeness. And then came the struggle against the Old [Presbyterian] Church machine,...then against Westminster, and then against the N.A.E. [National Association of Evangelicals], and gradually "the [separatist] movement" loomed larger and larger. Do not misunderstand me: my experiences here have convinced me more than ever that each of these struggles was needed and right; but the correct perspective got mislaid in the process...I wonder if that is not what happened to the Church of Ephesus in Revelation 2?
>
> ...I am sure "separation" is correct, but it is only one principle. There are others to be kept as well. The command to love should mean something... if I am to have that closeness to the Lord I wish to have, with its accompanying joy and spiritual power...
>
> ...God willing, I will push and politick no more....
>
> I am not sure as to what my future is...[1]

It was not until 1953 that Fran had fully worked it all out...

---

[1] Dennis, *Letters of Francis A. Schaeffer*, 37-9.

Chapter 12

Fran presented his findings in the summer of 1953 in a Bible camp. 'True Spirituality' or the Christian as a 'fruitful bride' were two ways he characterized his conclusions.

Ever thorough, Fran first explained the two main reasons why a believing Christian nevertheless failed to become a fruitful bride. Under the reason of 'ignorance' he listed five possible causes:

1. The Christian 'may have been taught how to be justified but never taught the present meaning of the work of Christ for him'.

2. The Christian 'may have been taught to become a Christian through the instrumentality of faith, but then he may have been left, as though from that point on the Christian life has to be lived in his own strength'.

3. The Christian 'may have been taught the opposite. That is, that having accepted Christ, in some antinomian way it does not now matter how he lives'.

4. The Christian 'may have been taught some kind of second blessing, which could make him perfect in this life when he receives it. This the Bible does not teach. And therefore he just waits hopelessly, or tries to act upon that which is not'.

5. The Christian 'may never have been taught that there is a reality of faith to be acted on consciously after justification. This last point is the point of ignorance of many who stand in the orthodox and historic stream of the Reformation'.[1]

Under the second reason, 'doctrine unpracticed', Fran used the example of justification.

In the last analysis it is never doctrine alone that is important. It is always doctrine appropriated that counts. We can see this in the case of justification. There are many men, unhappily, who have heard the gospel and know the gospel, but do

---

[1] Francis Schaeffer, *True Spirituality*. (Wheaton, Ill. : Tyndale House Publishers, 1971), 84.

not take Christ as their Savior. In such a case a man has the knowledge, but it means nothing to him, because he has not taken it...In justification we must see, acknowledge, and act upon the fact that we cannot save ourselves. In sanctification we must see, acknowledge, and act upon the fact that we cannot live the Christian life in our own strength, or in our own goodness...[1]

He went on to point out justification happened in a moment. However, sanctification was a life long endeavor and certainly not a mechanical thing like a certain prayers. Fran's outbursts of anger that plagued him were not so much sin as continual reminders that he lacked 'peace', 'self-control', 'patience' and perhaps other fruits of the Spirit. In any event, the Christian had to first reach the true spiritual life - the practice of sanctification - by three steps:

1. When...(I) accept Christ as...(my) Savior...(I am) immediately in a new relationship with God the Father...
2. When I accept Christ as my Savior I also come into a new relationship with God the Son. He is at once my 'vine,' my 'bridegroom'...if I, as a branch and as a bride, am not bringing forth the fruit one would expect from him...what is wrong?
3. When I have accepted Christ as my Savior, I am also immediately in a new relationship to the Holy Spirit. The Holy Spirit lives in me, as the agent of the whole Trinity. Now the fruit of the Spirit is clearly delineated in the Bible...[2]

And why then do we lack fruits of the Spirit? In one word: sin. Our sin has grieved the Holy Spirit, the agent of the Trinity. That was why sanctification was a never-ending process, although justification had already taken place in a moment. The weapon to battle sin was love. And the love should be demonstrated.

The world did not just step aside and wait for Fran to finish his spiritual struggle. A son, Franky, was born August 3, 1952. Franky's oldest sister Priscilla was 13. In 1953 the Schaeffers took a long 'furlough' in America. The daughters attended Stevens in Germantown. Priscilla would actually graduate from an American high school. Fran taught at Faith Seminary in Wilmington. Highland

---

[1] Schaeffer, *True Spirituality*, 84-5.
[2] Schaeffer, *True Spirituality*, 82.

College in California honored him with an honorary Doctor of Divinity degree. He also was guest speaker at numerous churches. In fact he spoke 346 times by Edith's count. Fran's new-found spirituality, called by some 'observational love', was misunderstood by many in his denomination. Was he preaching accommodation? Appeasement? Fran insisted he was preaching love in order to be sanctified. But many thought he had mellowed too much.

"The Mission Board is actually considering not sending us back to Switzerland," he told Edith.

Fran was tiring of the belligerence in his own church. Yet unbelievably another split occurred. Once again Carl McIntire led Fran and others into a new denomination, this one called the Bible Presbyterian church, later renamed the Evangelical Presbyterian church. The new denomination of course required a new seminary. This one was called Covenant Seminary and was located in St. Louis. Fran's church became ever smaller. Yet each time Fran supported its exodus because it was always triggered by some shift to modernism that he considered intolerable.

By the time the split was official, the Schaeffers were already back in Switzerland, starting something very unique. The idea erupted in January 1955 when Edith was reading Isaiah 2. "In the last days the mountain of the Lord's temple will be established as chief among the mountains; it will be raised above the hills, and all nations will stream to it."

Edith was jolted. "Surely God is encouraging us to host such a 'house of God' in the mountains of Switzerland!"

Fran was just as inspired by the insight. L'Abri, French for 'the shelter', would be a study center and refuge, especially for young people. However Fran later said the L'Abri Fellowship was not a work of evangelism but a work to demonstrate to current generations that God exists. This was the way Fran and Edith were living out 'True Spirituality'. In any event there never seemed to be any lack of young people staying at their chalet seeking answers. Many of the first visitors were brought there by Priscilla, now 18. Some were flippant but they truly wanted answers. At long last Fran could fully expound on secular culture from the Christian worldview. Certain ground rules were set to eliminate rancor. They would not discuss specific organizations, just ideas.

But Fran's Mission Board did not appreciate L'Abri. "They are cutting our support," a stunned Fran told Edith, "giving as their reason that we are no longer full-time missionaries."

In addition to that blow many letters were being written by Fran's fellow churchmen in America to churches around Europe that Fran had gone astray. His ideas were wrong, they warned. It seemed an astonishing turn of events just as he considered himself spiritually renewed. Then the world really struck the Schaeffers. They learned young Franky had polio! It was so ironic. To Edith, Franky had been maddeningly precocious, not only bright and outspoken but dashing about and climbing recklessly like a much older boy. Now he had polio, crippling one leg in particular! He would require much extra attention - including massages and exercises. About this time Susan was confined to bed from an attack of rheumatic fever. And then they suffered yet another blow.

"We are forbidden by the canton officials to return to Champery!" they gasped one day.

They had been doing too well at their evangelizing. To make matters worse if they did not have some other suitable location, with residence purchased by a specific date of March 31, they would have to leave Switzerland. What a turn of events. But just as amazing was their response. They trusted God completely. The Schaeffers calmly took out a map and planned their campaign. The descent by rail from Champery into the Rhone Valley and the ascent up the other side by rail brought them into the canton of Vaud. There above the village of Ollon, mirroring Champery on the other side of the valley was a cluster of five villages. One of these five was Huemoz. For almost exactly every penny they possessed and with just two days to spare they acquired a chalet in Huemoz. Chalet les Melezes was named for beautiful nearby larch trees. Everything fell into place so miraculously the Schaeffers seemed truly in God's hands. L'Abri was begun in Chalet les Melezes.

"To show our trust is complete we will resign from the Mission society," they announced.

Even though financial support was almost nonexistent Fran felt free at last. Edith was elated. Few were more qualified or more eager than she was to host seekers of the truth. Edith loved being a homemaker and hostess. The more guests, the bigger the challenge. Within two years L'Abri regularly hosted two dozen guests at the chalet. It certainly was not without cost to the Schaeffers. The onslaught of guests - soldiers, students, drifters - virtually used up every possession they had acquired over the years: sheets, rugs, dishes, curtains. And yet just enough funds trickled in to replace that which was lost. Edith wrote a L'Abri 'Family Letter' to more and more supporters. Edith enjoyed this task. She typed rapidly and composed easily. Her letters were long and detailed.

She joked, "I am not much good at condensing..."[1]

Soon she had 1000 sympathizers on her mailing list. She never asked for money, although the need was implied. She had much progress to report too. Within three years they housed guests in three chalets: Melezes, Beau Site and Chesalet. One of the very first guests had been a tall 19-year-old Swiss-American, John Sandri. John was cosmopolitan, having been born in Belgium and raised in Scarsdale, New York. He had been brought to L'Abri by a friend. Although he had attended church as a boy he thought Christianity was sugar-coated nonsense. L'Abri edified him. Only ideas were discussed. The taboo on organizations and personalities continued. Any idea was fair game as long as it was pursued to reveal its purpose to life. The Schaeffer children participated just like guests. Young Franky, perky even wearing a leg brace, joined in too. And the Schaeffers had visitors who had unparalleled knowledge of their subjects. Hans Rookmaaker spoke on art. C. Everett Koop spoke on medicine.

Fran, for all his fiery temper, could show amazing patience with seekers of truth. He didn't just lecture but he also sat for hours talking one-on-one or to small groups. Many had come to prove Fran wrong. Friday generally brought an influx of new visitors. They were oriented, then listened to lectures and discussions through the entire weekend. Fran conducted Sunday morning service. Sunday afternoon was highlighted by Edith's 'High Tea', a pleasant social gathering that tripled the size of the guests because it attracted so many locals. From Monday to Thursday Fran's ministry focused on Bible classes he taught on a regular basis in nearby villages and beyond. He had a class at a café in Lausanne. He also traveled miles northeast to Basel, still in Switzerland but hugging the Black Forest of Germany. Farther yet, he journeyed every other week southeast across the Alps to Milan, Italy. While Fran traveled to his Bible classes Edith ran the chalets and hosted guests.

The Schaeffers began to vacation in Italy. Fran and Edith knew they had to make occasions to be alone with the children. That was impossible at L'Abri. They especially liked the shore area in the vicinity of Genoa. They took walks, had picnics on the beach, swam in the Mediterranean, read to each other and enjoyed the local color.

---

[1] Schaeffer, *With Love, Edith*, 416.

They became attached to a small hotel in Alassio and its owner. Of course the children soaked up Italian like sponges. Even Franky soon rolled his r's. Not all the Schaeffer getaways were to the Mediterranean. Occasionally they would go up even higher into the mountains. Once they spent five days in a pension at a dizzying altitude of 8000 feet. In the mountains or on the Mediterranean reading aloud was a favorite recreation. Edith always tried to select the most entertaining of wholesome stories. If they were biographic, so much the better. So they read *Little House on the Prairie*, Laura Ingall's touching story of 19th-century life in America. They also read stories by Amy Carmichael, the missionary who founded the Dohnavur Fellowship in India. Amy's remarkable true story *Mimosa* was a favorite.

In August 1957 Priscilla married John Sandri in a white organdy gown made by Edith. The ceremony was in Ollon in a church so old it was already 400 years old when it reverberated from preaching of the great Swiss Reformer Farel in the early 1500's! The church was double-arched stone. It had only 17 pews with no center aisle. The organist played Bach for the wedding. Priscilla looked very much like Edith, dark-haired and sharp-featured. But although Priscilla looked like Edith, temperamentally she was like Fran, tense and edgy. It was Susan who was calm like Edith. After the wedding the newlyweds went to Lausanne, where both would continue their studies. After a year there they would go to St. Louis where John would enter Covenant Seminary. Priscilla had left a farewell letter to each member of the Schaeffer family - under their pillow!

In 1958 while speaking at Cambridge University in England some students tried to get Fran together with C. S. Lewis. At 60 Lewis was the most influential Christian writer of the century. He dwarfed theologians like Karl Barth and Paul Tillich. Lewis had only that year published a book on the Psalms, just one of his many popular books. Possibly millions of Christians owed their beliefs to Lewis's brilliant explanation of the faith in *Mere Christianity*, *Miracles* and *Problem of Pain*. Lewis also had a well-earned reputation for being a bruising, almost terrifying, debater. Lewis believed the Bible became historical with the appearance of Abraham. Everything before that might be mythical in his view. Calling a story mythical was not derogatory to Lewis. He loved myth and believed it contained great eternal truths. However, Fran considered the Bible historical right back to the creation. If only he could debate Lewis.

"But the meeting could not be arranged," he told Edith.

L'Abri had been established in England, although as yet its members had no physical facilities. One of the most enthusiastic students at Cambridge was a tall, red-haired South African Ranald Macauley. He was finishing his degree in law. But Fran had set him on fire. Now he wanted to study theology. He was soon visiting L'Abri in Switzerland. In the summer of 1959 Fran and Edith hosted 185 seekers at Huemoz for varying lengths of time. Visitors were from 16 different countries. Holland was enthusiastic for L'Abri too. They soon had a chapter there too. Fran and Edith now assumed they had an obligation to visit England and Holland yearly.

"If the funds are available," added Fran.

Almost on New Years Day in 1960 Edith's mother Jessie died of a heart attack at 85. Edith had not seen her in six years. Jolted by that fact Edith returned to America that same year - too late for the funeral but not too late to visit her 84-year-old father. God's hand seemed on the Schaeffers because while in America Franky was examined at the Pittsburgh Children's Hospital. An innovative surgeon there moved a muscle from the front of his crippled leg to the back. In time Franky would walk more normally.

In 1960 L'Abri opened their Farel House 'study center' to honor the great Reformer William Farel, Several hundred years before he had been chased out Huemoz by angry women throwing rotten potatoes! Ranald Macauley and the Druckers, a married couple from England, were instrumental in starting Farel House. All had independently asked to study at L'Abri half the day and work the rest of the day. The Schaeffers thought it was a great idea and dedicated the sunroom of Beau Site to the task. By November 1960 three students studied in that sunroom. Books were borrowed from the Evangelical Library of London.

The first hint of recognition by the secular press surfaced in the fall of 1960. A reporter from *Time* magazine arrived to interview the Schaeffers for four hours. Next day he and a photographer returned. The *Time* article came out in January 1961. Titled 'Mission to the Intellectuals', the article was essentially accurate but slanted to make the Schaeffers appear artsy, even elitist. One sentence read, "Each weekend the Schaeffers are overrun by a crowd of young men and women mostly from universities - painters, writers, actors, singers, dancers and beatniks - professing every shade of belief and disbelief..." Fran was quoted, "What we need is a presentation of the Bible's historical truths in such a way that it is acceptable to today's intellectuals. Now, as before, the Bible can be acted upon, even in the intellectual morass of the twentieth century."[1]

The article generated inquiries about L'Abri, although neither Schaeffer thought much about the article other than that it was basically correct. Fran was not satisfied with forever expanding the facilities at L'Abri anyway. He wanted to carry his message abroad. He had a compelling message to a desperate world. But he was sure he had to be presenting it not just to 30 or 40 listeners at L'Abri but to 500, 1000 or 5000 in great auditoriums. Then, God willing , he could get his message out in books to millions more!

But Edith did not want him to travel.

In 1961 Susan returned from studying occupational therapy at Oxford to marry Ranald Macauley in the same church in Ollon. Ranald was of Scottish descent, and even wore a kilt. Nine-year-old Franky wore a smaller version of the kilt at the wedding and asked to join the Macauley clan! Ranald and Susan would go to England, where Ranald was to study theology at London University. Susan also left a deeply personal farewell letter to each Schaeffer. It was becoming a family tradition.

About that time Udo Middelmann, a German who was studying law, came to L'Abri. Influx of high-powered students volunteering as workers at L'Abri triggered some ambitious projects. Newcomers were alarmed that Fran was 'throwing away ' his compelling lectures. Thus, they began taping. To be useful the tapes had to be carefully catalogued, preserved and copied for wide distribution. The new workers, enthused by Fran's message, were only too happy to take on the task.

Yet the success of L'Abri eventually created enormous tension between Fran and Edith…

---

[1] "Mission to the Intellectuals" in *Time*, 11 January 1960, 62-3.

Chapter 13

Edith loved everything about L'Abri. But she also worked slav-
ishly to keep it hospitable as well as caring for Franky. She expected
Fran to be there as often as possible to share the burden. He agreed
but became more and more excited as visitors, most at first hostile,
accepted his world view. Edith later described it:

> ...He has talked to beatniks, hippies, drug addicts, homo-
> sexuals and psychologically disturbed people. He has talked
> to Africans, Indians, Chinese, Koreans, Japanese, South
> Americans, people from the islands of the sea, from Australia
> and New Zealand and from all the European countries as
> well as from America and Canada. He has talked to people of
> many different political colours...
>
> In it all God has been giving him an education which it is
> not possible for many people to have. The answers have been
> given, not out of academic research (although he does vol-
> umes of reading constantly to keep up) but out of this arena
> of live conversation. He answers real questions with carefully
> thought out answers which are the real answers. He gets ex-
> cited himself as he comes to me often saying, "It really is the
> answer, Edith; it fits, it really fits. It really is truth, and be-
> cause it is true it fits what is really there."[1]

But finally Fran seethed over it. After an evening of success Fran
would vent his fury with Edith. Often he would pound the wall.
"People 'saw' tonight! Incredible how the lights came on for so
many of them...*But no one...is ever going to hear...no one*...except a
handful...What are we doing? What am I doing?"[2] He had to get his
message to a larger audience! Until he could get his message out in
books - a task that seemed very far off - he had to travel. Just
lecturing guests at L'Abri and teaching Bible classes within a day's
travel was not enough. He had to build contacts, reach multitudes.
So Edith relented on brief travels, often traveling with him but
complaining about being away from L'Abri. She reacted strongly at

---

[1] Edith Schaeffer, *L'Abri*. (Wheaton, Ill. : Tyndale House
Publishers, 1969), 227.
[2] Schaeffer, *Tapestry*, 537.

any talk of extended speaking tours. Fran lost his temper with greater frequency. He was regressing to his former low spiritual state. But during his travel he was energized.

Meanwhile L'Abri grew. The English L'Abri could now house searchers. Ranald and Susan had located a property near London. A separate chapel building in Huemoz was planned for 1965. In Huemoz the fellowship either owned or rented several chalets, including one called Tzi No. Next to Tzi No was the minuscule chalet called Mazot, where Priscilla and John Sandri, back from seminary in America, lived. John's duties were to teach French and copy tapes. Of course he was also a minister and studied at Farel House. In 1964, the third Schaeffer daughter married in the church in Ollon. Debby married Udo Middelmann. Udo was a German from Wurttemburg, a province that bordered Switzerland. Udo's father and mother had openly opposed Hitler during his 12-year reign of madness. Udo followed the path of John Sandri.

"To St. Louis where Udo will enter Covenant Seminary," announced Debby.

By the mid-1960's, the 'children' had certainly become less an immediate concern for Edith. The daughters were married. In fact Priscilla and Susan were mothers. Only Franky was not grown, yet he too was soon gone. Partly because of Franky's dislike of home study his education had been less rigorous than the daughters'. To receive an adequate education Franky had to be sent to a private school in England. Fran and Edith were relieved when Franky's first letters from England showed he was wildly enthusiastic about it. Franky had seldom known the company of boys his own age. Because Fran grew more and more frustrated about his restricted ministry, Edith relented more and more. One evening in particular jolted Edith. They were not at L'Abri with a young crowd but in Zurich with a group of older professionals. When the evening started the group was cynical, even hostile. Yet by the end of the evening Fran had completely won them over. They had dropped all coolness and asked questions as eagerly as children. Edith was overwhelmed with guilt. Fran did have a very powerful message.

'Oh, Lord, please forgive me if I have been piece of dirt in the water pipe!' she prayed. Eventually Edith was able to reflect, "In the very early part of the 1960s, I was going through a time that could only be described as self pity. I had begun to look away from 'willingness for anything' to a desire for 'something for myself,' and this filled far too much of my thoughts and prayer times. It was an elusive thing that could be rationalized as something I 'deserved'!"[1]

Fran set up increasingly grueling speaking schedules. Edith followed suit. She talked to female college students about love, marriage, sex and all the problems of being female in a changing world. She defended homemaking, insisting it took great creativity to raise a family, entertain guests and keep up a home. And she was direct about intimate things too. Her counsel was well received. She too had a worthy mission away from L'Abri. Soon she and Fran were at L'Abri in Switzerland only three months out of the year.

Fran's presentation was well-honed after more than 10 years of answering tough questions. He spoke at all major universities. For years evangelicals and Bible-believing Christians had been portrayed even by other Christians as backward hicks. Fran's exposition of art, literature and philosophy took many colleges by storm. He was still belittled by intellectuals - even some envious evangelicals - in print, but few wanted to join him in open debate. He was a deliberate, very sober speaker. And he was a respectful, patient listener. He completely subdued his volcanic temper. Most audiences quickly concluded this was a good man who really believed what he was saying. He asked nothing from them but an hour or so of their attention. His thrust in his series of talks slowly jelled into a book. His lectures at Wheaton College in 1965 became the 1968 book *The God Who Is There*. Critics complained cynically that his book was too spare, with not enough footnotes to substantiate his claims. They were disingenuous because they knew the scope of his argument would have required a volume far too large to ever publish.

"The danger is that people will take him for a scholar, which he is not," groused Mark Noll, an evangelical professor at Wheaton.[2]

An amazing thing happened to Edith at this time. During Fran's lectures she realized how out of touch she had become with his arguments. She had been too busy at L'Abri entertaining guests, keeping house, caring for Franky's special needs and doing a dozen other things! Now she was a listener, one of the most eager listeners Fran had. She listened avidly, scribbling notes. And all the steps of logic clicked into place for her. She certainly didn't need the

---

[1] Schaeffer, *Tapestry*, 520.
[2] Kenneth L. Woodward, "Guru of Fundamentalism" in *Newsweek*, 1 November 1982, 88.

argument to convince her of the truth of Christianity but she could use its power herself to convince skeptics.

To an upstart Christian publisher like Intervarsity Press, Fran was an opportunity. They suspected he was hot. And they were right. His books sold. They rushed his collected talks into print. Some overlapped. Much was redundant. Much was missing. His writing was often labored and convoluted, a far cry from the lucid prose of C. S. Lewis. But from 1968 to 1972 Fran published 13 books with Intervarsity Press and Tyndale House. The first year alone he issued two very important but somewhat overlapping apologetic books, *The God Who Is There* and *Escape From Reason*. The gravity of his subjects certainly had not diminished by 1971, because that year he published his third major apologetic book, *He Is There and He Is Not Silent*, as well as his inspiring work on sanctification, *True Spirituality*. The following year brought his fourth main apologetic, *Back to Freedom and Dignity*, in addition to two major Bible contributions, *Basic Bible Studies* and *Genesis in Space and Time*.

Fran never tired of emphasizing the importance of the historicity of Genesis 1 through 11, "In some ways these chapters are the most important ones in the Bible, for they put man in his cosmic setting and show him his peculiar uniqueness. They explain man's wonder and yet his flaw."[1]

Fran now had a sizeable readership. He became the champion of some evangelical circles - the champion who could hold his own against intellectuals. C. S. Lewis, the former undisputed champion, had died in 1963. Many academics who disagreed with Fran did not dismiss him as a Bible-thumping fundamentalist either but regarded him as a worthy opponent. By 1973 he had spoken at the powerhouse universities of Princeton, Harvard, Yale, Oxford and Cambridge. He had the credentials to be taken seriously. Attracted to Fran's 'camp' were Jack Kemp, Jerry Falwell, Chuck Colson, Bill Bright, Pat Robertson, Cal Thomas and many other notable 'conservatives'. They were entranced with the power of his message. For Fran had no use for the much overused concept of 'leap to faith', which nonbelievers equated with 'blind faith'.

Fran emphasized, "Christianity is to believed because it is historically true!" Lewis and J.R.R. Tolkien argued the same fact.

---

[1] Francis Schaeffer, *Genesis in Space and Time*. (Downers Grove, Ill.: InterVarsity Press, 1972), 9.

Edith's participation in Fran's travels was short-lived. By the end of 1965 she had returned to L'Abri to care for Fran's mother Bessie. Grandmother Schaeffer moved to L'Abri because at 85 she required constant care. Fran was an only child. No one else - but Edith - could assume the responsibility for Bessie. Of course Edith had help but her ministry was once again mainly running L'Abri and writing 'family letters'. She also intended to write a history of L'Abri. Meanwhile Fran traveled and lectured.

Fran's main argument for Christianity was put forth in three books. *The God Who Is There* is a very lengthy introduction of the argument. *Escape From Reason* overlaps the introduction but also extends the argument. *He Is There and He Is Not Silent* concludes the main argument. Fran traced the way the way people through the generations - whether theologians or philosophers - have tried to answer the basic questions about reality.

"In other words, how did they seek truth?"

From earliest times, Fran asserted, mankind argued ideas in the same way. If one answer was deemed correct, its opposite was deemed incorrect. Mankind also accepted that there were absolutes. And in general mankind realized there was a greater power - a supernatural power. That began to change in the 13th century with the Catholic theologian Thomas Aquinas. Aquinas embraced the pre-Christian philosopher Aristotle, who had been out of favor for centuries. Aristotle favored reason above all. Mankind was very self-sufficient in his opinion. According to Fran this made Aquinas and many in Christendom - only the Catholic and Orthodox churches were in existence at this time - begin to assert human authority. Although Aquinas was quite pious himself he had opened the door. Mankind became increasingly independent or 'autonomous'. The Bible diminished as the ultimate authority.

"Early 'modern scientists'," continued Fran, "presupposed that the universe was created by a reasonable God and because of that they could investigate the universe using reason."

But from the works of the English physicist Isaac Newton and the French philosopher Rene Descartes in the late 17th century was born 'modern modern science'. To them the universe was a machine with *no outside influence*. The system was closed. Rationalism was born. Mankind could observe particulars and with his reason make universals out of the particulars. This method of 'empiricism' or 'evidentialism' was the method Aquinas used, except *now God was excluded*. This, according to Fran, was a step backward but still correctable with the proper methods of seeking truth.

But in the 18th century the French philosopher Jean-Jacques Rousseau ushered in 'naturalism'. Mankind, according to him, had not benefited from religion, culture and science but instead had been corrupted. Mankind had to go back to nature or his natural state. The result, insisted Rousseau, was absolute freedom. But Fran insisted the result was not just anarchy but the loss of universals. Without universals there could be no presuppositions. Without presuppositions one can scarcely reason.

Fran was sure thinkers prior to Rousseau would have lamented, "Don't you see what you have done? Where are the universals? How are you going to know? How are you going to build enough universals out of particulars even for society to run, let alone build true knowledge, knowledge that you really know, and are sure that you know?"[1]

Meanwhile in the late 18th century, in *Critique of Pure Reason, Critique of Practical Reason* and *Critique of Judgment*, the German philosopher Immanuel Kant wrestled with the problem of a closed system. How does one explain immeasurable concepts like 'meaning' and 'value' with a materialistic rationalism that can only observe and measure? This dilemma of a closed Godless system set the stage for the most radical change of all. Up to this time mankind had always thought in terms of 'antithesis': A is A, and A is not non-A. These were steps in classical logic. In antithesis if one thing is true, then its opposite is not true.

According to Fran, "'Antithesis' is the classical methodology of epistemology, or 'knowing'."

But it was the German philosopher Hegel in the early 18th century who concluded only too well that antithesis was not providing all the answers. In other words Hegel questioned the method of truth-seeking rather than the assumption of a closed system. So he decided to change the method of seeking truth! Instead of using antithesis, he proposed 'synthesis'. One concept remained a thesis and the other an antithesis, but he did not choose one or the other but something in between! The answer was always a synthesis.

---

[1] Francis A. Schaeffer, *He Is There and He Is Not Silent*. (Wheaton, Illinois : Tyndale House Publishers, 1971) in Schaeffer, Francis, *The Complete Works of Francis A. Schaeffer: a Christian Worldview*, v. 1. (Westchester, Illinois : Crossway Books, 1982), 311.

Then in the mid-19th century came almost the final blow from the Danish philosopher Soren Kierkegaard.

"He is the father of modern secular thinking and of the new theological thinking," concluded Fran.[1]

Kierkegaard correctly realized a synthesis could not be defended by reason. But instead of backtracking to the classical thesis/antithesis way of reasoning he defended his synthesis by a 'leap of faith'. By the beginning of the 20th century all serious philosophical thought in Europe was divided into two hopeless camps. There was the materialistic concept for things that could be measured. But removed from immeasurable truths like value and meaning these truths were sterile and meaningless according to its skeptics. The other hopeless camp was Kierkegaard's concept that was used for love, faith and other immeasurable truths. Kierkegaard's skeptics judged his search for truth that required a 'leap of faith' illogical and hopeless.

"I call the line, the line of despair," wrote Fran of the moment in time Kierkegaard's concept was generally accepted.[2]

Yes, the acceptance of Kierkegaard's concept brought total despair. The false methods of modernism had doomed the pursuit of truth in philosophy and theology! As a result modernism became characterized by existentialism. Since reason is hopeless all one can do is exist and experience. Certain undefined feelings like dread, or 'Angst', are present too. Modernism is a dreary dead-end. Logical positivism was an attempt, mainly seen in the work of Ludwig Wittgenstein and Bertrand Russell, to rescue thinking from the morass. Fran believed this method too was flawed because it has no presupposition.

"It puts forth no theoretical universal to validate its very first step," concluded Fran.[3]

Unfortunately the sad state of philosophy spread to other disciplines. Fran documented the onset of despair in art - exemplified by the increasingly unrecognizable forms in post-impressionism and 'modern' art. Fran admitted the despair in music was harder to document, but believed it culminated in modern jazz. Others might have seen the culmination in hard rock music. Under the envelope

---

[1] Francis Schaeffer, *The God Who Is There*. (Downers Grove, Ill.: InterVarsity Press, 1968), 22.

[2] Schaeffer, *The God Who Is There*, 15.

[3] Schaeffer, *The God Who Is There*, 25.

of 'general culture' Fran included literature, exemplified by the anarchy and pornography of novelist Henry Miller, as well as modern poetry that is not poetry at all and angry destructive plays. Within the general culture, what Fran considered perversions like homosexualism and abortion became more and more acceptable. Everywhere people who were looking for truth found nothing but despair and, very often, destruction. And Fran was certain all these failures could be traced to one underlying cause: *the flawed modern way of seeking truth by synthesis*.

"A way which had been unthinkable to educated man before this," was how Fran described this flawed method that also brought down theology![1]

The culmination of the destruction of theology was in the existential works of Karl Barth. Nothing could be proven, according Barth. One merely leaped for faith. Barth's acceptance by the general theological intelligentsia opened the floodgates. Joining the ranks of modern theologians supposedly seeking the truth, then ultimately leaping blindly at faith, were Paul Tillich, Reinhold Neibuhr and Bishop John Robinson among Protestants. Catholics were led astray by Teilhard de Chardin, Karl Rahner and Hans Kung.

Fran postulated that using synthesis, the flawed way of seeking truth, for the truths in theology eventually ends one of three ways. Many of the lines of despair ended in Nihilism. The seekers of truth concluded life had no meaning. All was chaos. Mankind was just a fluke, no more than a smart animal. A second end was simply accepting a hopeless Dichotomy: the loftier things in our existence - like love and personality - are irrational; the material things in our existence have no meaning. Fran used the term 'upper story' for the loftier things and 'lower story' for the material things. His point was that one who sought truth by synthesis could not go back and forth between the two stories - except by a leap of faith. The third end to seeking truth in theology by synthesis was modern mysticism.

At this point in his exposition Fran raised the point, "How then is historic Christianity, the view that continues only among the Bible-believing Christians, different?"

Yes, challenged his skeptics, just how is Bible-believing Christianity different?

---

[1] Schaeffer, *The God Who Is There*, 52.

Chapter 14

"First of all," Fran brusquely argued, "people who say all religions around the world are the same are either ignorant or liars!"

Only the Jews, Christians and Muslims, he explained, had a personal God. But unfortunately many modern Christian theologians have concluded God is not personal, using instead of 'God' gobbledygook like 'Ground of Being'. Some have even tried to reconcile their warped Christianity with Hinduism! Next Fran pointed out firmly that Christianity is not true because it is the best theological theory for righteousness. Christianity is true because *it happened.* The Old Testament of the Bible said that it would happen. The New Testament recorded that it did happen.

"Modern theologians however do not accept the Bible as fact," he noted.

How then to prove Christianity to those who do not accept the truth of the Bible? It was the same problem C. S. Lewis tackled in *Mere Christianity.* Fran used the presuppositional method, although he decried restricted nuts-and-bolts apologetics. He especially disliked bickering over methodology, because he was often accused of combining presupposition with the method of verification. Verification started from one or more hypotheses. The question was often raised: did Fran start from presuppositions or did he start from hypotheses?

"Let's not waste time bickering over it. Let me present my case."

First, Fran confronted the problem of existence itself, which raised these questions: Why is there something, rather than nothing? Why is the universe structured and ordered? Why is mankind so unique? To these questions, he responded, there are only three possible answers: the world came from nothing, or the world came from an impersonal source, or the world came from a personal source. The claim that everything in the universe flowed from absolutely nothing was as absurd to Fran as it had been to the apostle Paul in Romans 1:20. How could any serious, thoughtful person believe the world came from nothing? The second alternative, an impersonal beginning to the universe, was the position favored by liberal theologians, pantheists and many scientists. Fran insisted an impersonal source could not create 'personality'. Some countered that 'personality' is simply an illusion. Fran argued that no person actually lived that proposition. No person - unless insane - really believes he is not a person.

"A personal source endowed not only personality but purpose and direction," Fran insisted.

Secondly, Fran confronted the 'mannishness' of mankind as well as the 'dilemma' of mankind. Humans are unique. They are diverse and gifted - loving, inspiring, moral, rational, artistic - yet capable of great cruelty too. Moreover they seem incapable as a whole of harmony, suggesting they are insufficient in themselves. Fran rejected the humanistic notion that mankind was basically 'good'. The evidence of mankind's cruelty had never been stronger. The 20th century was a time of staggering atrocities like the Holocaust. Many atrocities where humans killed *millions* of fellow humans - Cambodia, Russia gulags, India, Rwanda - scarcely caused a ripple in the rest of the world! Fran argued that man's cruel nature could be traced to his origin.

"And there would be no notion of good or evil nagging at us if we started from an impersonal source," he pointed out.

A personal source certainly did provide an answer. But it left more than one possibility. Perhaps mankind was created intrinsically cruel by a creator that was cruel. Another possibility is that mankind was created intrinsically good, but mankind chose to go bad. Such was the basic outline of what Fran was arguing in his three books: *The God Who Is There, Escape From Reason* and *He Is There and He Is Not Silent*. To those who were confused and lost he offered a solution: Christianity. Believing in a cold, impersonal universe governed only by chance was a recipe for suicide. All of his later books he said had to be plugged into these three books. They were the framework. Anyone reading any of his subsequent books without reading the first three was starting three feet off the ground! In the three books Fran had written only about 150,000 words, with much redundancy. So critics quickly jumped on the fact that much of his development was skimpy. His history of 'thought' amounted to a mere three percent of the verbiage in Will and Ariel Durant's well-known history of civilization.

"Are they interested in a product or a conclusion?" asked Fran's defenders.

Fran was totally convinced he was right. And he convinced many others. The evidence of the decline of both secular and religious thought was rampant, especially in the 1960s. Shallow thinkers like the pundits on television blamed the chaos in America on the Vietnam War. But the root cause was much deeper. Popular culture debunked the Bible. Universities offered vague relativism. Youths sought answers to the meaning of life in sex and drugs. Fran was never more alarmed. While he worked incessantly to get his message out Edith did the same with her works.

L'Abri, her history of the fellowship, was published in 1969, although she had finished the manuscript several years earlier! Now she cogitated over how to edit voluminous correspondence she had created and distributed since 1948. And there was also the matter of their personal life. Perhaps there was a book there too. And her facility for counseling led to a regular column for *Christianity Today* magazine. Beginning in 1971 she would submit a column every two weeks.[1] Family responsibilities were always there too. Grandmother Schaeffer had been in Edith's care for six years! Finally in 1971, at 91, Bessie died.

"Grandmother's life here has gone by, *our* years are going by..." wrote Edith wistfully.[2]

Soon after his mother's death Fran had a brainstorm while hiking in the mountains with Edith. He felt like Charles Wesley who once yelled, "Paper! Ink!" when a hymn popped into his head. Fran would consolidate his teachings into a book called *How Should We then Live?* Moreover, he would attempt something he had never done before. He would present his idea in a series of films. The series would be in response to Kenneth Clark's immensely popular television series in 1969 called *Civilization*. Clark was a humanist and atheist. Clark had taken a survey of the same culture that Fran had surveyed and had come to the conclusion that man was indeed quite an admirable success! Clark grudgingly voiced admiration for the eastern religions - probably because they were so impersonal - but religion was scarcely necessary for mankind's fabulous accomplishments. In America the Public Broadcasting System brought *Civilization* - with implied approval of its message - into homes all across America.

"*Civilization* affirmed the humanistic message that man is great," grumbled Fran.

---

[1] These abruptly ended in 1977 but a compilation was published in 1977 by Fleming H Revell Co as *A Way of Seeing*.

[2] Edith Schaeffer, *Dear Family: The L'Abri Family Letters, 1961-1986*. (San Francisco: Harper & Row, 1989), 177.

Many felt Fran, with his great knowledge of art and philosophy, was the only one who could properly respond to Clark from the Christian worldview. The title of the series was taken from the King James Version of verse 10 of Ezekiel 33: "Therefore, O thou son of man, speak unto the house of Israel; Thus ye speak, saying, If our transgressions and our sins be upon us, and we pine away in them, how should we then live?"

How Should We then Live? would be produced by none other than son Franky. Franky and Genie Walsh had also been wed in the Ollon church in the summer of 1970. In 1975, artistic and energetic at 23, Franky seemed a perfect choice to produce the series. *How Should We then Live?* became a 10-part series of Fran's interpretation of the 'success' of mankind. Over six months they filmed in America, Switzerland, Holland, Belgium, Germany, France, Italy and England. They filmed in public squares, cathedrals and museums. Fran's message was that philosophy and 'modern modern science' did not have the answers and never would have the answers.

"But Christianity does have the answers."

The series, released in 1976, was not the success of Clark's *Civilization* but it did bolster many faltering Christians. And it did make Christians aware they could confront the arts and philosophy. They did not have to rely on a 'leap of faith' or 'blind faith'. Those were red herrings. The truth behind Christianity was historical and real. It was the same point C. S. Lewis had made so eloquently in print during the 1940s and 1950s. Fran followed up the series with an 18-city speaking tour and a book that would be published in 1976. In addition to detailing the corruption of modern culture - including Alexander Solzhenitsyn's exposure of the miserable failure of Communism - Fran also had a very ominous warning.

"If Christians feel they can sit on the sidelines, if they do not speak out for their beliefs in an increasingly Godless society some day they will be considered the *enemies* of that Godless society - even in America!"

Many were shocked now when they saw Fran. He had gone to Europe in 1948 in his typical dark suit and tie, with his face clean-shaven and thinning hair slicked straight back. Now he wore long stockings, knee-length hiking knickers and an open necked shirt. His page-boy hair covered his ears. His chin sported a bushy goatee. However, during speaking tours and protest marches he often donned a dark suit again. He also warned about the danger of a recent development: abortion. In 1973 the Supreme Court ruled in the case *Roe versus Wade* that women had a constitutional right to have an abortion during the first six months of pregnancy. The floodgates to mass murder opened. The abortionists used the language devilishly. The baby was called a *fetus*, as if it were not a person. The woman who had the abortion was not against anything; she was *pro-choice*. The people who opposed killing babies called themselves *pro-life* but their opponents, including the press, labeled them *anti-abortionists*. Fran was not fooled by the phony rhetoric.

"But how can we stop this sick development?" he lamented.

The year 1977 was dismal for the Schaeffers. Two men very close to the hearts of Fran and Edith died. Hans Rookmaaker had been only 56. Franky was crushed too. "I can't believe it. He was so young. He was so alive...He helped me as young artist, from the time I was twelve..."[1] Then Edith's father George Seville died at 101. Back in America she attended his funeral. The graveside ceremony hit her very hard because she felt like she had never really observed her mother's passing. Then, still in America, the Schaeffers got word the chapel at Huemoz had burned! Nearly everything was destroyed. It would take two years just to repair the organ.

"It certainly seems like Satan is trying to stop us," said Edith.

To help people understand suffering she wrote *Affliction* that same year. In June 1977 the Schaeffers' old friend, C. Everett Koop, spoke at L'Abri. Koop had founded a medical journal on surgery for children. He was internationally known as a man of medicine. Koop warned about increasing insensitivity in America to death. There was increasing sentiment to do away with all who were 'unwanted': young and old. It smacked of Nazi mentality but America seemed unaware of this. The Schaeffers, including Franky, were ignited.

"We must make a film series on this threat!"

But Fran and Dr. Koop had to articulate their arguments first. That would result in a book. Fran, the prophet who should have been immune to shock, was horrified by the easy acceptance of abortion - murder of one out of three of the most defenseless in society - by the public and by what seemed to be inevitable beyond abortion. If babies could be murdered because it was expedient how long would it be before the elderly were murdered? After all, many elderly were 'unwanted', the buzzword of abortionists. Fran collaborated with Dr. Koop on *Whatever Happened to the Human Race?* The book outlined the atrocities of abortion - which exposed

---

[1] Schaeffer, *Tapestry*, 595.

just how inhumane the humanists really were - and what it meant: the public was being prepared for 'mercy killing' of the sick and elderly. Fran and Dr. Koop tried to rally support:

> People are special and human life is sacred, whether or not we admit it. Every life is precious and worthwhile in itself - not only to us human beings but also to God. Every person is worth fighting for, regardless of whether he is young or old, sick or well, child or adult, born or unborn, or brown, red, yellow, black, or white.
>
> If, in this last part of the twentieth century, the Christian community does not take a prolonged and vocal stand for the dignity of the individual and each person's right to life - for the right of each individual to be treated as created in the image of God, rather than as a collection of molecules with no unique value - we feel that as Christians we have failed the greatest moral test to be put before us in this century...[1]

Then they filmed *Whatever Happened to the Human Race?* The five 50-minute episodes - all directed by Franky - were on abortion, infanticide, euthanasia, apologetics for finding the truth, and the Bible itself. Locations were in America, Austria, Switzerland and Israel. Fran was awed by Israel, where they shot scenes from the north in Galilee to the south at the Garden Tomb.

Fran gushed, "Franky has enabled me to preach the Gospel more clearly in this fifth episode of the film than I have ever been able to do in my lifetime. It is so complete. I am thankful it [the film] can go on speaking."[2]

Surprisingly, Fran's comment had a poignant touch of finality to it. He had been losing weight during filming, so he consulted a doctor. Fran was diagnosed as having an enlarged spleen. Edith decided to call a doctor friend at Mayo Clinic in America. Then, in October 1978, just 36 hours after filming *Whatever Happened to the Human Race?* was completed they experienced, as Edith wrote later, a change "as great this month as Alice in Wonderland's change as she fell through the rabbit hole..."[3]

---

[1] Francis Schaeffer (with C. Everett Koop), *Whatever Happened to the Human Race?* (Old Tappan, NJ: Fleming H. Revell, 1979) in *Complete Works*, v. 5, 409.

[2] Schaeffer, *Dear Family*, 391.

[3] Schaeffer, *Tapestry*, 289.

Chapter 15

Fran and Edith traveled to Rochester , Minnesota, optimistically believing Fran would get his Mayo Clinic 'checkup' at St. Mary's Hospital, then rush back to his hectic schedule after a one-week delay at most. But concern over his enlarged spleen evolved into concern over swollen lymph glands in his neck. A gland was biopsied. One morning Fran told Edith the results.

"The gland is malignant, and the lymph system is involved," he said grimly.[1]

Malignant! Cancer! Edith was reeling. Calmly Fran phoned his son and daughters, then took a CAT scan and a bone marrow test. Debby and Franky soon arrived from Switzerland. Debby praised God that He assured believers that in the end victory was certain.

They prayed over Psalm 71 with the poignant line, "Even when I am old and gray, do not forsake me, O God, till I declare your power to the next generation, your might to all who are to come."

'Don't let any one of us stop trusting You, Lord,' prayed Edith, 'please may we be *real* in our love for You, and in our wanting to be in Your will, and in our victory over whatever Satan would be trying to do to us now. Please Lord give us present victory in the heavenly battle. *This* is the time that counts for Your glory Lord - don't let us flub it.'[2]

But results of Fran's tests were grim. Fran at 66 had lymphoma. A mass of lymph nodes behind his intestines was as large as a football. He even had cancer in some of his bone marrow. Treatment would be intense: six months of chemotherapy in 21-day cycles, with five days of the chemical followed by 16 days of rest.

"There will be no return to Switzerland," someone muttered.

Through the financial help of friends Edith secured a three-story townhouse. Visiting off and on were the four 'children'. Fran rejoiced that his family drew around him in such a trying time. He was already taking his first chemotherapy. The period of chemicals was not as bad as he expected. He was merely weak. The 16 days of rest however brought great fatigue and stomach pain.

---

[1] Schaeffer, *Tapestry*, 613.
[2] Schaeffer, *Tapestry*, 615.

Edith provided Fran comfort. They both loved classic English mystery writers. So Edith read aloud Agatha Christie, Dorothy Sayers, Ngaio Marsh and others. Occasionally she would read one of their favorites from childhood like *Penrod and Sam.* But nothing was more comforting than prayer. Letters, phone calls and telegrams demonstrated that thousands of others were also praying.

At the end of the first cycle Dr. Pettit said Fran was definitely improving. His blood was more normal, and the glands, even the nodular mass, had shrunk. The second cycle resulted in even more improvement. The Schaeffers were buoyed with optimism. Fran and Edith began enjoying Rochester - even evangelizing. Often Fran would speak after showing one of his films. One talk drew 1600.

Then unbelievably the doctor could detect no lymphoma. "If I were looking at your present CAT scan without knowing your history, I would think it to be that of a perfectly normal situation."[1]

They left Rochester in March 1979. All that was required for the near future were checkups. Fran pointedly told the press that his 'recovery' was not because he had greater faith in God than anyone else. Regrettably many who had just as great a faith in God did not recover. Fran rushed back into his schedule. Soon he accompanied the film and book versions of *Whatever Happened to the Human Race?* to England, Sweden, Australia and 20 cities in America.

In Massachusetts Fran developed shingles. Shingles was a viral disease that caused pain on the skin. Shingles often occurred in people with weakened immune systems. Edith was sure Satan was attacking from all fronts because of Fran's *Whatever Happened to the Human Race?* and its powerful message. In spite of shingles Fran continued. After the first 10 cities Fran and Edith were more convinced than ever that America must be alerted to a growing culture of death.

Fran said, "I know we must keep on, and that these Seminars are more important than we realized. I have a fire in my bones."[2]

But by the time Fran finished the 20-city tour he had become pessimistic. Opposition to the seminars was strong. Turnouts were low. Was it already too late? The grim result of the tour was mirrored by Fran's physical condition. In August 1979 a checkup at the Mayo Clinic revealed lymph nodes were enlarged in Fran's neck. He began chemotherapy again. He insisted Edith go to

---

[1] Schaeffer, *Dear Family,* 302.
[2] Schaeffer, *Dear Family,* 314.

Cambridge University in England as his substitute for a scheduled lecture. On her return in December she found Fran's condition worse. Chemotherapy was increased.

On May 31, 1980, exactly 49 years to the day after Fran walked onto the Sydney-Hampden campus as a freshman the college honored him. Fran's life work seemed at a summation point. For Crossway Books he wrote *A Christian Manifesto*, a book that summed up a Christian's civic duty. He stressed how humanism, which proudly admits to no purpose in life, had gained the upper hand in America - so much so it was even defended by liberal theologians like Martin Marty. "Wake up! Strengthen what remains and is about to die..." from Revelations 3 was Fran's clarion call.

Fran had written over 20 books. Some were out of print. Crossway Books agreed to publish his complete works in five affordable volumes. The groundwork for all Fran's work was the trilogy of *The God Who Is There*, *Escape From Reason* and *He Is There and He Is Not Silent*. All his other books, he insisted, "fit into these as spokes of the wheel fit into the hub."[1] Every book was re-edited. Fran was quick to point out the unifying theme of all his work was 'the Lordship of Christ in the totality of life'. Passages were updated, even clarified. An appendix titled 'The Question of Apologetics' was added to *The God Who Is There* to satisfy numerous requests. The target date for publication was 1982. The set was titled *The Complete Works of Francis A. Schaeffer: A Christian Worldview*. Fran's life work totaled about 2000 pages that contained over one million words!

Edith too was busy with books. She was a prolific writer. In one 'Family Letter' she explained, "I find it important to treasure the shiny days of life and the glowing half days, or one-hour periods of time, or even five special minutes. A fence should be put around such times in our memories to protect them from being blurred by the next storms that hit! It is important not to forget what the Lord has given along the way."[2]

And that she did. In a 1981 'Family Letter' Edith revealed why she had been 'unavailable' for months, even at various L'Abri sites:

> ...I have been writing *The Tapestry*, a 600-page book which will be published by Word Publishing House...While struggling with the thought of not wanting to write a biography about Fran and myself and our lives and work, the thought

---

[1] Schaeffer, *Complete Works*, v. 1, x.
[2] Schaeffer, *Dear Family*, 366.

emerged, "Why not write a book that weaves something of history together with glimpses of people's lives and the glimpses of God's plan, recognized in often short flashes of understanding, along with glimpses of crucial choices made the close working together which changed the direction of life for one - then for thousands of other people affected by that one?"

...It is an encouragement to be reminded that God is God indeed and that He does have a pattern, not a deterministic one, but a marvel that only He can understand of the effect of choice, the choice of one person after another, yet the reality of His weaving steadily, the wonder that the loom has not been demolished. There is a meaning to history, and the pattern is continuing, history is going somewhere![1]

By now Edith had written numerous books. Fran said they were an integral part of his own life work. The key books were *L'Abri* and *Tapestry*. But much remained for Edith. Her 'Family Letters' were an integral part of the Schaeffers' life work too. To appreciate the task of editing the letters one had to realize that since 1947 Edith had written about 50,000 words a year! By the end of 1982 her words totaled nearly two million! This was a task that awaited her in the future. For she and Fran were still busy fighting his cancer and speaking out as often as they were able.

"Dr. C. Everett Koop has certainly added to his prestige as a spokesman against abortion, infanticide and euthanasia," marveled Fran in January 1982.

President Reagan had appointed Dr. Koop America's Surgeon-General. Democrats in Congress who wanted no opposition to abortion fiercely opposed him with the preposterous lie that he was not qualified. But Dr. Koop's credentials as a man of medicine were overwhelming. His appointment was approved. And he did not relinquish his fight against abortion. In the summer of 1983 two rallies were going on at the same time: one in Atlanta and one in London. In spite of threats and bad health Fran gave a memorial service in Atlanta for fourteen babies who had survived vicious abortions but died later.

"These tragic victims of inhumanity at least received death certificates to attest they were human," Fran stated bitterly.

---

[1] Schaeffer, *Dear Family*, 329-30.

Thanksgiving 1983 back at Huemoz was a turning point in the Schaeffers' life. Fran sat at the head of the table and helped serve turkey, dressing, cranberry sauce and rolls. He ate very little himself though.

"That night he became very ill...," Edith remembered later.

Fran alternated between bouts of sweaty fever and teeth-chattering chills. After six days of this draining sickness his doctor had him taken to a hospital in Aigle. There the Schaeffers were told Fran had to get expert care immediately. Through the help of friends Fran was flown to the Mayo Clinic in Rochester. All the while, unbelievably, he was trying to finish a book he called *The Great Evangelical Disaster*. It would eventually be added to Volume 4 of his completed works. The book detailed disastrous consequences of accommodation in the evangelical churches. They had been the last barriers to the onslaught of humanism and atheism. But beginning about 1900 they began to back off the great strengths of evangelicalism: Biblical inerrancy and the right kind of truth-seeking. By 1936 when Machen was defrocked by the Presbyterians the victory of humanism was almost complete.

Fran's book *The Great Evangelical Disaster* was yet another mani-festation of his rallying cry. "Wake up! Strengthen what remains and is about to die..."

In Rochester the diagnosis was grim. Fran's lymphoma had re-gressed into a much more dangerous kind. In addition he was hemorrhaging. Half his colon had to be removed. Yet, after that surgery he began recovering. He asked Edith to buy a house in Rochester. They would have to do their L'Abri work near the clinic. He couldn't be rushed across the ocean every time he had a setback. Shortly after Fran turned 72 on January 30, 1984, Edith flew back to Switzerland to pack their belongings. Of course the chalets in the Huemoz area would remain occupied by L'Abri. Packing complete, Edith - after living in Switzerland for 35 years - returned to Amer-ica. She was stunned to see that Fran had finished *The Great Evan-gelical Disaster*, had been released from the hospital and was ready to go to a conference!

"To promote the book," he explained.

But he was very sick when he returned to Rochester from the conference. He went into the hospital where he worsened. By Easter Edith had to summon the children. Fran knew what was happening. He calmly asked Edith if she intended to remain in Rochester after his death. When she answered 'yes' he said he would like to be buried there. His last request was to be moved into their new house. So they moved a hospital bed and necessary medical equipment into the family room. Fran was moved there May 5. He could see into the yard. Trees were budding. Squirrels and birds darted about. Fran was delighted. Edith had his favorite music playing at all times: Schubert, Bach, Beethoven, Chopin and Handel. And in his last days Edith and the children were with him around the clock.

Sunday morning, May 13, Fran watched James Kennedy preach against Marxism on TV. He was pleased, murmuring, "Keep on...keep on...from strength to strength."[1]

Fran continued to weaken. At one point he had just enough strength to pray, "Dear Father God, I have finished my work. Please take me home. I am tired."[2] Just after midnight on May 15 Edith and the others read Fran the *Daily Light*. What would seem uncanny coincidence to unbelievers was gratefully accepted by the Schaeffers as a gift from God. The first quotation was from Revelations 21:4:

> He will wipe every tear from their eyes. There will be no more death or mourning or crying or pain, for the old order of things has passed away.

More quotes from various books in the Bible followed. All attested to the victory of Christ over death. Edith could only console herself with the fact that she would see him again. She was so thankful she and Fran believed the Bible's inerrancy. She did not have to agonize over whether a passage was God's word or not. No doubt gripped her as she saw Fran's very tired face turn to wax. He was with God. He actually desired that. 2 Corinthians 5:8 said so: 'We are confident, I say, and would prefer to be away from the body and at home with the Lord.'

At 4 AM May 15, 1984, Francis A. Schaeffer had taken his last breath.

---

[1] Schaeffer, *Dear Family*, 388.
[2] Scott R. Burson and Jerry L. Walls, *C. S. Lewis & Francis Schaeffer*. (Downers Grove, Ill.: InterVarsity Press, 1998), 43.

Chapter 16

American President Reagan praised Fran as "one of the great Christian thinkers of our century, with a childlike faith and a profound compassion for others....his life touched many and brought them to the truth of their Creator."[1]

Billy Graham said, "He was truly one of the great evangelical statesmen of our generation...More than virtually any other thinker he had keen insight into the major theological and philosophical battles of our time."[2]

Life without Fran was daunting for Edith. Still, her father lived to be 101 years old. Her mother lived to be 85. Edith was a mere 69. Edith persevered. She would live nearly another 30 years. She was very productive for the next 16 years in Rochester, even founding a L'Abri chapter there. She acted as a Trustee for the larger L'Abri organization. In addition she wrote more books, the chief of which was the result of editing family letters. Publishing all the letters over nearly four decades was not practical. That would have required up to 5000 pages. The work had to be split into two books even after deleting over 80 percent of the content. In 1988 Edith published *With Love, Edith*, letters from 1948 through 1960. In 1989 *Dear Family*, letters from 1961 through 1986, came out.

She had more books in her head. She was eager to record her love for China. She did that with a children's book titled *Mei Fuh* in 1998. She followed that with *A Celebration of Children*, a book about children, in 2000. Edith planned to write a book titled 'Full Circle'. At the onset of the new millenium however, Edith at 85 had seriously slowed. She resigned as a Trustee for L'Abri. She nevertheless endured, moving back to Switzerland to be near family. She first resided in a small studio apartment by Lake Geneva near Vevey. About 20 miles southeast was Huemoz where L'Abri was run by daughter Priscilla and husband John Sandri. Later Edith moved to Gryon, near her daughter Debby and husband Udo Middelmann. In her last years, caretakers from America helped her remain relatively independent, although she was in a wheelchair.

Edith Rachel Merritt Seville Schaeffer died March 30, 2013, at 98.

---

[1] Parkhurst, Jr., *Francis Schaeffer*, 217.
[2] Parkhurst, Jr., *Francis Schaeffer*, 27-28.

***

Other than the numerous worthy books by Francis and Edith Schaeffer as well as two commendable scholarly biographies of Francis in 2008 and 2009 [1], the legacy of the Schaeffers has suffered in the 21st century.

The real day-to-day administration of L'Abri Fellowship had passed on to others during Fran and Edith's frantic schedule his last 15 or so years. John and Priscilla Sandri had been in Huemoz many years. Udo and Debby Middelmann lived in the Gryon L'Abri. In Europe major 'residential branches' of the fellowship were also established in Holland, Sweden and England, the latter founded by Ranald and Susan Macauley. American branches of the fellowship were in Southborough, Massachusetts, and eventually Rochester. Residential branches could room and board students. In addition the fellowship established 'resource centers' in various countries to provide information for visitors.

According to some observers L'Abri Fellowship in Switzerland has degenerated into retreats for well-to-do drifters and non-think tanks of vaguely-defined postmodern scholars. If reportage is reliable, current residents have little respect for Fran and Edith Schaeffer. John Sandri supposedly said, "Schaeffer didn't read books. He got his material from magazines. *Newsweek, Time* - he'd take them to the beach." As one writer observed, Sandri's views are a "telling expression of what L'Abri has become."[2] Few involved with the Swiss L'Abri in the 21st century profess to the Calvinist beliefs held by Fran and Edith Schaeffer. The supposed decline of L'Abri nevertheless hardly stirs a ripple on the sea of Christendom, and only mildly rocks the legacy of Fran and Edith Schaeffer.

Such is not the case with son Frank Schaeffer. He definitely has damaged the legacy. Fran promoted Frank into a key position - arguably a prime example of inept nepotism - well beyond Frank's skill as a media craftsman at the time in producing *How Should We*

---

[1] Barry Hankins, *Francis Schaeffer and the Shaping of Evangelical America.* (Grand Rapids, MI: Eerdmans, 2009). Colin Duriez, *Francis Schaeffer: An Authentic Life.* (Wheaton, IL: Crossway Books, 2008).

[2] Both quotes from Molly Worthen, "Not Your Father's L'Abri" in *Christianity Today* (March 28, 2008).

THE SCHAEFFERS

then Live? and *Whatever Happened to the Human Race?* His achievements after he lost his father's coattails were by his own admission "mediocre".[1] His direction 'created' four embarrassingly clumsy movies. In the last of the four clunkers he for the first time was credited 'Francis A. Schaeffer', possibly hoping to capitalize on his father's reputation. He fell so low for a while he took to shoplifting.

His faith in those years floundered. He flirted with Catholicism, then settled on Greek Orthodox in 1990 (since abandoned although he still likes the pomp). By 1992 his failures at career and faith plus festering resentment of his mother led to writing and publishing *Portofino*, a blatant fictionalized study of his own family. His treatment of Elsa, who he admits is based on his mother Edith[2], portrays her as a hyperactive religious looney who also engages in infidelity. His sisters are either angry or meek - but always silly. In *Portofino* Frank was easier on his father, who is merely a religious looney with a volcanic temper. Frank is present as young Calvin Becker, unceasingly witty and delightfully mischievous.

Portofino was well received by those who love to hate Protestants and in particular Fundamentalists. Reviewers praised the boy Calvin's 'insight'. He was charming. He lifted the human spirit. They lamented the pitiful fact that the Becker parents tried to solve their 'all-too-human foibles' with the Bible. They called the Becker parents 'zealots' with 'narrow views', shuddering that their 'harshness and violence' were real. In short, the Franky-like Calvin was wonderful. His Schaeffer-like family was outright dangerous.

Frank disingenuously denied *Portofino* portrayed the Schaeffer family. Frank was simply using a technique long used by fiction writers. He took a situation he knew intimately and spun a tale from it. Certainly one of Franky's aims in the novel was to attack Protestantism and express admiration for sacramental religion. He wrote *Portofino* just after he had converted to the Orthodox Church. In *Christian Activist* he stated, "In the conflict inside the Becker household we find in a microcosm the larger story of the American experience. The Beckers are inventing their beliefs in a vacuum cut off from historical Christianity."

Frank had really found his cashcow. In 1997 he published *Saving Grandma*, a portrait based on Grandmother Schaeffer. The fictional grandma is a foul-mouthed matriarch who skewers Fran and Edith.

---

[1] Schaeffer, *Crazy for God*, 355.
[2] Schaeffer, *Crazy for God*, 19.

Zermatt, third in the trilogy, was published in 2003, a patchwork of Calvin indulgences and weakest of the cashcow trilogy.

Ever resourceful Frank, realizing *Zermatt* had exhausted the fiction but that the fiction trilogy raised public curiosity about just how much of his 'fictional' lampooning the Schaeffers was factual, decided he would at last tell the 'truth' (as well as glopping a fresh coat of paint on the cashcow). In 2007 he published *Crazy for God.* Frank tells the 'true story' of Fran and Edith Schaeffer in the spirit decried by William Blake: 'A truth that's told with bad intent beats all the lies you can invent.'[1] Frank, who is a gifted gossip, is superb with this technique. But a reader could argue Frank has another arrow in his sling: the half truth. This he wields with deft nastiness. Add yet another arrow: lies Frank throws about like confetti, gossipy nonsense he has heard along his convoluted way..

Crazy for God sparked great interest and partisanship in its readers. His father Francis, according to Frank, was a mixed-up, suicidal abuser. Most disturbing to friends of Fran and Edith Schaeffer was the heartless depiction of Edith. Frank asserts that he is even-handed with his mother. But for every complement about her he batters her with ten derogatory comments. Edith by Frank's pen is a snob. A bigoted snob. A bigoted snob obsessed with fine clothing and jewels. A bigoted snob obsessed with fine clothing and jewels who espouses outlandish ideas about sex. A friend describes Frank's treatment as "deeply dishonoring, monstrously ungrateful."[2] Frank even tried to incorporate slams by his sisters Priscilla, Susan and Debby, 69, 66 and 62 in 2007. Their replies show a cautious acquiescence to Frank.[3] Susan declined anyway. Priscilla was diplomatic, pointing out to baby brother how his upbringing was so much more challenging than theirs. Only Debby, if the reader can trust Frank's editing of the sisters' responses, praised her father but then took the opportunity to vent on Edith (age 92 at the time).

> My mother's legacy was in stark contrast [to father's positive legacy], as she singlemindedly pursued her ideals, often blinded to the realities of life or of our lives. As a dreamer and a highly artistic individual my mother created her own

---

[1] William Blake's poem 'Auguries of Innocence'.

[2] Os Guinness, "Fathers and Sons: On Francis Schaeffer, Frank Schaeffer, and Crazy for God." in *Christianity Today,* 2008.

[3] Schaeffer, *Crazy for God,* 38-43.

life with passion and hard work. I compare her to early discoverers of the North Pole. She pursued her objectives with determination, though bits of bodies all around her were lost to frostbite. The havoc she caused to all around her, as they were dragged in to help her meet selfimposed deadlines and goals, was phenomenal and scarring to me as a child. The force of her personality was such that I, at least, never even thought of refusing. Also, I would say, that though my father taught me the love of the Real, my mother's idealism has taken years to peel away.

So there was the sibling confirmation Frank wanted. He is not alone in his low opinion of Edith. Still, some might think he was ungrateful, so he spins stories about how much his mother Edith loved his books. She begged for signed copies to give her friends, claimed Frank. So, as Fran once supposedly pummeled tiny Edith behind closed doors, son Frank pummeled her in front of the world.

Of his sisters and brothers-in-law, Frank's wife Genie supposedly said, "They just don't like each other."[1] And perhaps not many others. Frank claims he and his sisters loathed Americans and pretended not to speak English if they encountered any such common people while in Europe. The American Midwest is to Frank "in the vast, nondescript middle."[2] He loathes the Swiss too, who traded "security for the lives of Jews they turned back to the Nazis."[3] The English were overbearing, self-anointed elites. Frank hated his grandmother Schaeffer and teased the elderly invalid mercilessly. He also detests Ralph Reed, James Kennedy, James Dobson, Pat Robertson, Jerry Falwell and Billy Graham. Some of them are said to have organized the Religious Right. Frank knows that he and his father did that.

Frank's truest thought in *Crazy for God* may be "I must have been insufferable."[4]

In *Patience with God* published in 2009, Frank (in his own mind) destroyed both evangelicals and militant atheists. Eventually in the book he condescended to impart the real truth about God. The book is a one-note whine. As a commercial success it was as shaky as *Zermatt*. What was Frank to do next?

---

[1] Schaeffer, *Crazy for God*, 302.
[2] Schaeffer, *Crazy for God*, 248.
[3] Schaeffer, *Crazy for God*, 26.
[4] Schaeffer, *Crazy for God*, 226.

He did what sells.

He dragged Edith out again for his next book. The book *Sex, Mom, and God* published in 2011 was a commercial success. Again, brilliant repartee spews from 10-year-old Frank. Never mind that in other books he laments in self-pity how at that age he was neglected, dyslexic and virtually illiterate - all of course caused by mother Edith. Again he hammers James Dobson, Pat Robertson, Jerry Falwell and Billy Graham. Frank invokes his father to ridicule these men. It seems in private Francis would rant that these very men were 'idiots'. To his very long hate list Frank adds homeschoolers, Sarah Palin, Pope John Paul II, Glenn Beck, George W. Bush, Franklin Graham, Elizabeth Anscombe and Malcolm Muggeridge. Although Muggeridge died in 1990, Frank changed him from "Dad's friend" in *Crazy for God*[1] in 2007 to "a rabid Far Right" Roman Catholic[2] in *Sex, Mom, and Go* in 2011.

But 97-year-old Edith bears the brunt.

Frank tells all about her love affair with a visitor to L'Abri, one that he admits was not consummated. Her beau is rich, sophisticated and sensitive to women. According to Frank, his mother thought her beau was the perfect love. Frank tells the reader this beau was by no means Edith's only infatuation. To Frank his mother led another kind of 'double life'.[3] She loved art and literature, which Frank deems very non-fundamentalist. That was her good side. Of course her bad side was her fundamentalism. So according to Frank's logic that made his mother a hypocrite. Frank states his mother also revealed her low opinion of evangelicals. She once blurted, "those so-called writers of the American Evangelical world who can barely speak English..."[4] Another time she supposedly spouted, "Pay no attention to those Evangelical idiots."[5] On the other hand Edith's attempts to explain something biblically fell into what Frank calls a 'wacky theological myth'.[6]

In *Sex, Mom, and God* Frank also brags about his sexual exploits as a teenager, satisfaction of a lust implanted in him by who else? Edith. By explaining sex to Frank when he was a child she perma-

---

[1] Schaeffer, *Crazy for God*, 340.

[2] Schaeffer, *Sex, Mom, and God*, 137.

[3] Schaeffer, *Sex, Mom, and God*, 91.

[4] Schaeffer, *Sex, Mom, and God*, 193.

[5] Schaeffer, *Sex, Mom, and God*, 194.

[6] Schaeffer, *Sex, Mom, and God*, 92.

nently inflamed him with desire. She also confided to Frank how his father had to have sex every night. Frank explained, "By eight or nine I was thinking like a somewhat horny twelve-year-old".[1] Was it any wonder at 15 he was having sex with visitors to L'Abri? Beautiful visitors too, he brags. All-knowing, tell-all Frank even treats readers to revelations about Martin Luther's sex life.[2] He reveals Luther had pre-marital sex with his future wife Katharina.

By 2012 Frank hinted he was no longer Christian, although he still attended church. Was it just another attention-seeking gimmick? Frank's latest incarnation is as a basher for politicos. He has moved beyond bashing only his mother and other evangelicals to a steady stream of rants about big business and the Republican Party. He repeats old fabrications of oil companies suppressing electric cars and other tales. But he has added rants against the Tea Party and Michelle Bachmann and anyone else who disagrees with his mercurial beliefs. He continually drops names implying he was once at the center of power, even a creator of the Religious Right.

Considering Frank's history, he might very well swing in yet another direction. There just might be a trilogy of 'self-revealing' books there for yet another cashcow. In the meantime Frank steadily chips away at the legacy of his parents, Francis and Edith Schaeffer.

THE END

---

[1] Schaeffer, *Sex, Mom, and God*, 32.
[2] Schaeffer, *Sex, Mom, and God*, 58.

Made in the USA
Las Vegas, NV
12 May 2024

89850418R00075